# MODERN **LIVING**
## WITH
# **FENG** SHUI

P9-BJQ-719

**ALBERT LOW**

# MODERN **LIVING**
# WITH
# **FENG** SHUI

Pelanduk
Publications

Published by
**Pelanduk Publications (M) Sdn Bhd**
(113307-W)
12 Lorong SS13/3E, Subang Jaya Industrial Park
47500 Subang Jaya, Selangor Darul Ehsan, Malaysia.

Address all correspondence to
**Pelanduk Publications (M) Sdn Bhd**
P.O. Box 8265, 46785 Kelana Jaya
Selangor Darul Ehsan, Malaysia.

Perpustakaan Negara Malaysia    Cataloguing-in-Publication Data

Low, Albert
    Modern living with Feng Shui / Albert Low.
    ISBN 967-978-649-8
    1. Feng-Shui. 2. Geomancy. I. Title.
    133.3337

Printed by Laser Press Sdn Bhd.

This book is specially dedicated to
Joanne and Wisely Low

# Contents

# 1.  Land Shapes

A London doctor by the name of Weston once observed that people whose names began with the first eight letters of the alphabet lived longer than the others.

Why these things should be so, and the reason behind it, have been the subject of much speculation. In feng shui, when you buy a house, you take into account the direction the house faces and its surroundings. But an important aspect for the geomancer is the shape of the land on which the house sits.

### The Perfect Square
This perfect shape with its sides equal in measurement, symbolises a land of wealth and stability. Good for the down-to-earth who is in pursue of material gains.

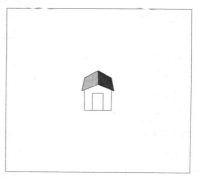

### The Rectangle
Symmetrical and balanced at both ends, this land shape will benefit the ambitious person who climbs his way up the ranks. Promises good prospects for politicians and those in the armed forces.

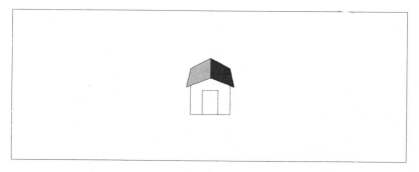

### The Circle

Also known as the Heavenly Shape. As the circle has no beginning and no ending, its perfection in all aspects renders it ideal for those seeking spiritual goals or enlightenment.

### The Bucket

Also known as the Gold Shape. The back portion is always smaller than the front. A large opening in the front would encourage luck and wealth to come pouring in. With its smaller back, the wealth that flows in will be trapped within that shape. This shape is beneficial for bankers and stockbrokers.

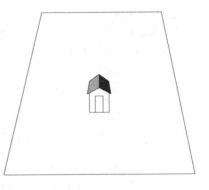

### The Horseshoe

This shape by itself suggests that it draws luck like a magnet. This unusual shape would only suit those who like to live in the fast lane where they deal with high volume of stocks, or for those who make their living as professional gamblers.

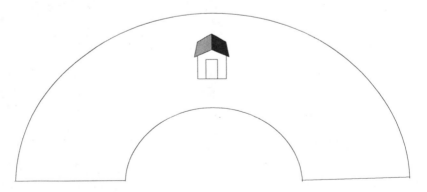

### The Shield

A shield is created when a house is built with its back against the steep side of a cliff. With the back portion thus guarded, full strength is concentrated on the front of the house. Good for those who have stepped on the shoes of others. This shape will protect them from any vulnerability.

### The Valley

The wind is rather strong when it passes a valley, so this is not a good site for your house. This may bring about instability in your job, business or family life, due to the presence of the wind that sweeps its way through.

Generally, there are five shapes representing each of the elements in their purest form, the rectangle represents the earth element and the square is for wood. An oval symbolises metal; a circle denotes water; and a triangle represents fire.

3

### The Arrow

An arrowhead-shaped land denotes a weapon of war, bringing bad luck and sickness.

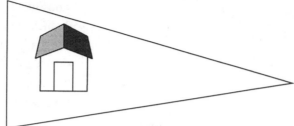

### The Triangle

A plot of land in the shape of a triangle is known as "Fire Land". Normally, you find such shapes of land at corners. In feng shui, this particular shape is very unpredictable because fire can be difficult to control. Quarrels and unhappiness may result.

### The Knife

Land in the shape of a chopper spells trouble for the family, both at home and in business. Be wary of the sharp edge of the "knife".

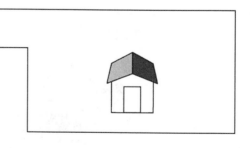

### The Boot

Staying on land in the shape of a shoe indicates being stepped on by others. This is particularly bad for businessmen, corporate leaders and politicians.

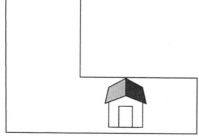

## The Fan

A plot of land shaped in a semi-circle is known in feng shui as the fan-shaped land, because it is but half of a full circle, it is deemed unlucky because such a shape is unable to collect the forces of *chi*. A home built on such land would be deprived of vital energy, and so its occupants would suffer misfortune and poor health.

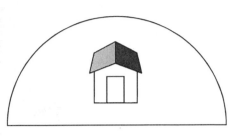

## The Snake

Snake-shaped land refers to land that is not on even level. Viewed from the side, it appears to be a snake raising its head to strike. Such land normally brings bad luck.

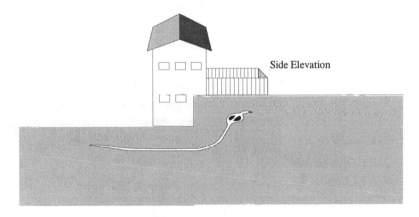

5

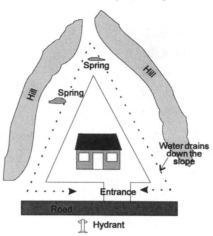

## The Triangle Sandwiched by Spring Hills

A triangle-shaped land represents the "fire" element and this spells bad feng shui. In normal circumstances, such a shape would create a lot of disharmony for the family. The occupants are unlikely to find peace of mind or success in business ventures.

However, in this case, the fire element is brought under control by the two springs which sandwich the house and help to cool down the land.

A word of caution, though. As long as the springs do not run dry, you are fine. Otherwise you might find problems queuing up at your doorstep.

## Surrounded by Water

If a plot of land is not landlocked has an access road and is surrounded by a river and a stream (*sui*), it is considered as having good feng shui.

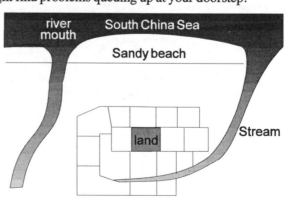

6

# 2. Horns (Deflector of *Sha Chi*)

I n Knossos, Crete, the ancient ruins of the Minoan Palace include a dilapidated fresco wall with a series of pictures. One depicts a young man with arms out-stretched, holding the horns of a ferocious charging bull and another shows him somersaulting over the beast's head.

In an interview, rodeo riders in Texas, United States, said such a stunt would be impossible to perform. Perhaps this daredevil act is a lost art which disappeared when the Minoan empire ended around 1250 BC.

Today, however, it is not unusual to hear the expression "take the bull by the horns" (to do something difficult in a brave and determined manner).

Marauding Vikings would stud their helmets with bull horns in the belief that they would be able to channel the strength of the dead animal into their mortal selves. This grotesque attire, accompanied by fearsome war cries and the flashing of swords, was bound to petrify their enemies.

In Vatican City, the Michelangelo masterpiece of a marble statue of Moses depicts Moses with two horns protruding from his head. Why did Michelangelo "adorn" Moses with the horns? Research shows that horns symbolise god-given power.

The horns of the velvet deer are treasured as an aphrodisiac by the Chinese, though this belief has met with scepticism in the West. On one occasion, a British royal in Hong Kong was told that consuming ground deer horns would promote health and longevity. He burst out laughing, and said that if it were so, ground table legs would have the same effect.

The spotted deer, also known as the sika deer, sheds its antlers in the fall and grows new ones in spring. The newly grown horns are soft covered with fuzz and rich in blood vessels. Before the velvet horns harden in summer, the Chinese collect these antlers. Sliced into paper thin wafers, they are sold at high prices to Chinese pharmacies.

In Russia where there are plenty of deer, scientists have carried out experiments in which a substance called pantocrine was extracted from deer horns, and fed to mice. It was found that his enhanced the stamina of the mice. Similarly, when this substance was given to 50 young men running in a 3km race, it was discovered that there was an increase in their endurance.

During the Ming dynasty, one of the emperors even ordered an expedition to Sumatra to hunt for rhinoceros whose horn was believed to be an elixir of immortality. Since then, this beast is still being hunted for its solitary horn which is believed to contain medicinal properties.

At Polonia Airport in Medan, Indonesia, the roof of the airport terminal is shaped like bull horns. Some Sumatra tribes also have the roofs of their huts shaped like bull horns to show that they are a hunting community. At the same time, the horns are supposed to ward off evil spirits. On the lighter side, horns also act as lightning conductors.

Carnivorous animals have sharp canine teeth to kill prey in order to survive. But for herbivorous animals such as the goat, deer, bull and rhinoceros, nature has bestowed antennae-like horns. Those protruding horns are sharp like spears and could prove lethal if they find their way into a victim's body.

Today, after animals are slaughtered for their meat, their horns do not go to waste. Instead, they are made into ornamental objects, and sold to tourists who consider them exotic items.

In feng shui, the sharp end of the horns are believed to emit chi. According to a Chinese saying, poison is used to neutralise the poison. So bull horns and deer antlers can be used as deterrents of negative forces and *sha chi*.

# 3. Secret Arrows

The proper word for destructive *chi* is *sha chi*. This is normally created from sharp corners and pointed roofs of buildings. Some *sha chi* is man-made, while others are created by nature. Because the destructive shapes that cause *sha chi* are not normally noticed by the layman, they are often known as the "secret arrow".

Secret arrows that carry *sha chi* normally 'attack' in a straight line. When a house, building or office stands in their way, these premises absorb their negative vibrations and thereby suffer from bad feng shui. For example, a businessman would find that if his business premises face a secret arrow, he may end up suffering huge losses of wealth.

A politician facing a secret arrow may be betrayed by his colleagues and comrades. And the typical healthy person living under such conditions may find that his health has deteriorated somewhat as a result of the influence of *sha chi*.

**Types of Secret Arrow**
**Secret arrow from below:** Even though this house (see diagram) sits comfortably at a vantage point on top of a hill, its feng shui is still badly affected as the secret arrow from below, in the form of the roof structure of the house on the lower level, destroys its harmony.

**Neutral**: These houses face one another; the sharp points caused by their roof-tops are both pointing upwards, and therefore have no effect. In this position, the houses are said to have neutral secret arrows.

**The Goliath**: This arrow-like building, typically larger than those around it and found in commercial districts, cuts across the neighbouring building and destroys its neighbour's good feng shui.

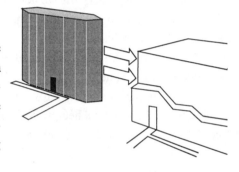

Sometimes secret arrows or *sha chi* can be found in many guises. Since they cannot be identified by the untrained eye, many times the unsuspecting occupants of the home or business premises fall victim to its harmful effects without even knowing what hit them. Several common examples of these "invisible secret arrows" are shown below.

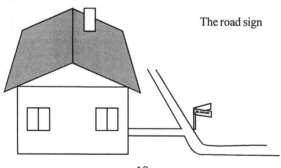

The road sign

## 3. Secret Arrows

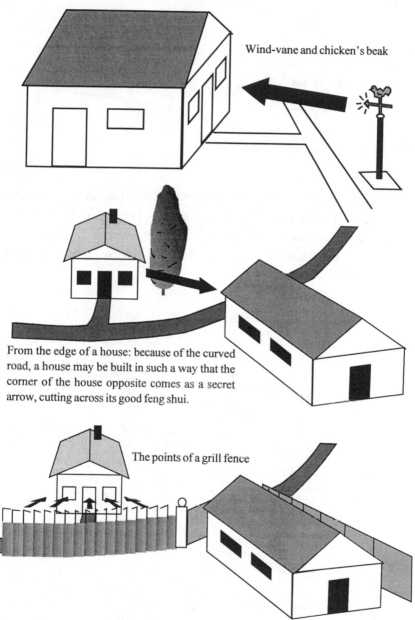

Wind-vane and chicken's beak

From the edge of a house: because of the curved road, a house may be built in such a way that the corner of the house opposite comes as a secret arrow, cutting across its good feng shui.

The points of a grill fence

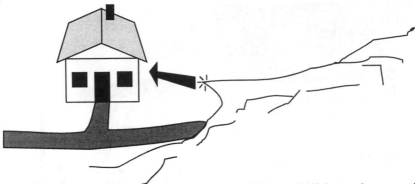

**From nature:** There are times when houses which are built in rural areas end up facing secret arrows due to natural formations. These secret arrows coming from hills and mountains are usually formed by weathering. The *sha chi* that emanates from them destroys whatever good feng shui is brought about by the rest of the surroundings.

# 4. Enhance the Feng Shui of your Home

**L**et us look at the various ways of enhancing the feng shui of your home.

## Gold

The rich sometimes lay gold ingots as part of the foundation of their home. Those who are less wealthy may sprinkle some gold dust or place old coins in the foundation. This is based on the belief that money makes money. So a good foundation with gold as part of it should augur well for the house.

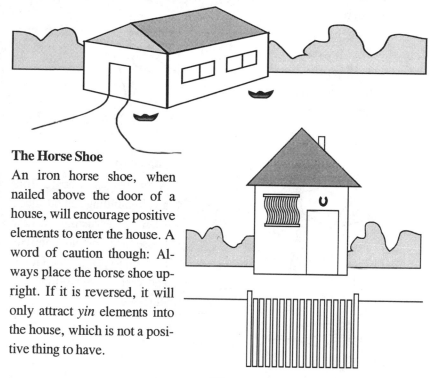

## The Horse Shoe

An iron horse shoe, when nailed above the door of a house, will encourage positive elements to enter the house. A word of caution though: Always place the horse shoe upright. If it is reversed, it will only attract *yin* elements into the house, which is not a positive thing to have.

### Antlers

Antlers left on both ends of the roof-top is believed to guard the house and keep off intruders.

### Heavenly Dragon

A Metallic dragon with one hand raised, attached to the weather vane which placed on the roof-top is considered a symbol of the heavenly dragon. This dragon is considered all-powerful and is believed to keep away mischievous spirits.

### Old planks

A few planks of board from an old building can be added when constructing a new house, as these old materials are said to protect the family and keep off misfortune and illnesses.

14

# 5. The Roof

**T**he roof of a house is similar to the hat on a person's head. Such a "hat" has to be well-designed and placed, otherwise imbalances would bring bad feng shui to the household. Let us look at some designs and their effects.

**Well-balanced**: Enhances the feng shui of a house.

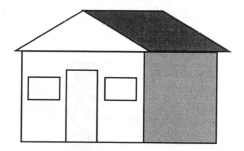

**Slanted**: Whichever side the roof slants, it would erode the occupant's fortune.

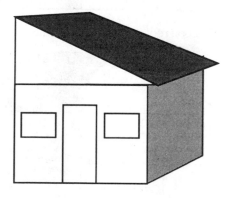

**Big Front, Small Back** A roof that is high in front but tapers down to its end symbolises that one is successful in the beginning but towards the end his fortune would diminish.

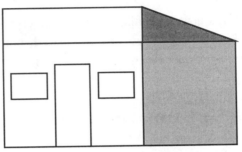

**Quarter Coin** A quarter shape can hardly contain *chi*, so to have such a shape for the roof would not do much good; it would affect the vitality of the occupant.

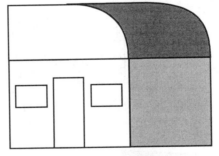

**Half Moon** The half moon roof is of the metal element, suitable for people in the armed forces.

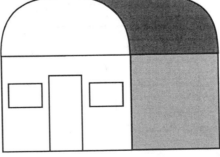

**Well-balanced Roof** The feng shui of this house in enhanced by its well balanced roof.

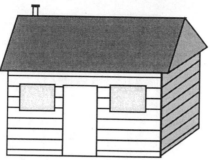

**Oversized Roof** A roof that is too large for the house creates bad feng shui. It symbolises that one would always be at a disadvantage.

**Horn Roof** A house with horn-like roofs would "dissect" a house. The family would be divided.

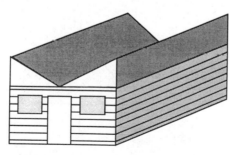

**Flat Roof** A building that has two storeys or more should not have a flat roof. Such a "prominent" building should have a proper roof otherwise bad feng shui will result.

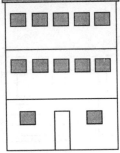

**Round Roof** A circular roof without beginning or end is a form of perfection, normally used by religious orders.

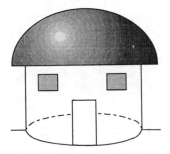

**Pyramid** A pyramid roof is called the mysterious roof. Its four sides face the cardinal points of a compass, mysterious forces are likely to be channelled in. Such a roof serves the mystics.

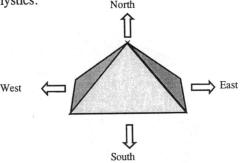

**Imperial**: A larger version of the heavenly roof. Apart from temples, it is used by imperial palaces.

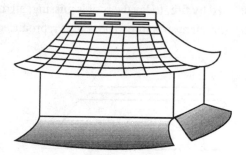

**Cone**: Suitable for clock or bell towers.

**Heavenly**: The front of the roof and its sides are curved. Winds would be directed upwards, thereby causing no damage to the structure. Such roof is normally found on temples, thus known as the heavenly roof.

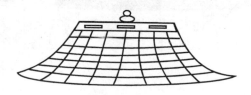

**Ming Fort**: this ancient fort still stands at the foot of the Purple Mountain in Nanjing. Backed by a hill with walls on both sides, the fort was impenetrable at that time. Destroyed by fire, today the roof is missing; all that is left are the walls of a once magnificient structure. The roof is reproduced in the illustration here.

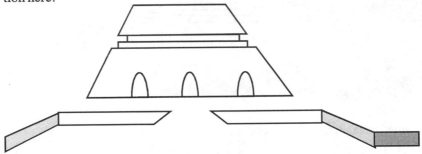

**Imperial Hall**: A carved stone gourd or a pagoda sits on the roof as a talisman to protect the building. This design was used by the first Ming emperor, Hong Wu. Known as the Beamless Hall because no beam was used. The building has now been converted into a memorial hall for soldiers.

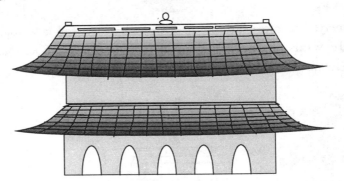

## Missing Roof

A house with half a roof creates an imbalances in feng shui. The best thing to do is to build the missing half of the roof. But if you cannot afford that, use solid material such as wood to build the skeleton of the other half of the roof.

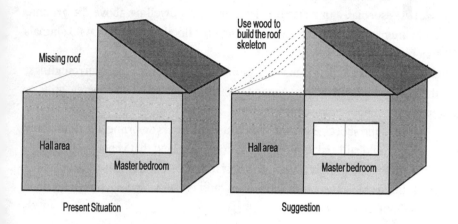

# 6. On Stilts

**H**uts sitting on wooden stilts are a common sight in many rural areas, especially in Asia. By elevating one's dwelling above the ground, there are natural advantages to be had against floods and hungry wild animals that roam the forest at night.

While these thatched huts are built in harmony with their surroundings, the same cannot be said for concrete houses which stand on concrete stilts or are partly supported by concrete stilts.

Due to the shortage of land or because the site is on prime location, many people would still risk building their homes on land that is not properly levelled. In the study of feng shui, it is best to build your house on a flat piece of land. Let us look at some of the houses built on stilts, and see how they stand where luck is concerned.

## Weak Back

A bungalow with its back portion resting on stilts has negative feng shui. It symbolises a lack of backing for all the occupant's undertakings. Hence success is hard to come by.

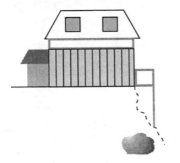

## Supported Balcony

It is not so bad if only the balcony is supported by stilts. Such a house would not bring bad luck to the occupants.

## Half Supported

If half the house is supported by stilts, than half of its luck hangs in limbo.

## Three quarters on Stilts

A house with three quarters of its base resting on stilts, can only hold on to one quarter of the luck that comes its way, since only that portion is on steady ground.

## Fully on Stilts

A bungalow that sits fully on stilts brings ill luck to its occupants as it has no solid base for support. Businessmen should never live in such a house as they risk losing all the wealth they have accumulated.

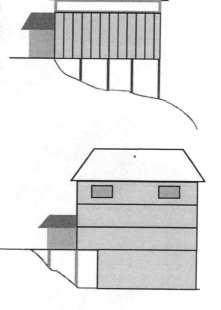

## Weak Front

A house will have a weak front if that portion is held up by stilts. Most of your plans are likely to go awry since you will not project a good first impression to business associates.

# 7. The Front Porch

Typical of Malaysians, we like to renovate our home — bedroom, kitchen, living room, backyard — you name it, we have done it.

The porch, being part of the front façade of the house, is also a favourite spot for home improvement. For good feng shui, the porch should be in proportion to the house and the driveway. If the porch is extended too far thus making it out of proportion to the house, then there would be an excess of *yin chi*, which destroys good feng shui.

**Half Covered**
Covering only half the driveway, this balance allows adequate lighting and ventilation. Good feng shui.

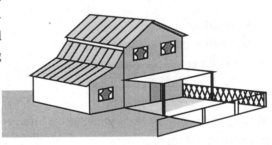

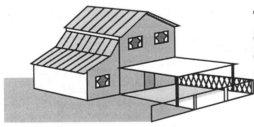

**Three-quarter Covered**
Such porch also allows adequate lighting and ventilation. Good feng shui.

## Driveway Covered

A porch that is totally covered brings darkness to the front entrance of the house. Too much *yin chi* here, bringing bad luck to the occupants of the house. Bad feng shui.

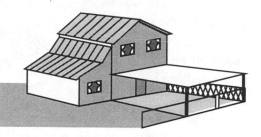

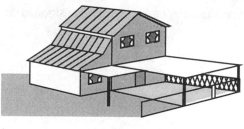

## Garden Covered

A porch that shades not just the entire driveway but part of the garden as well also creates too much darkness. Bad feng shui.

## All Covered

This is the worst kind of extension as everything in the garden and driveway will be dark, out of balance with the light of day. Bad luck and ill health to the occupants. Extremely bad feng shui.

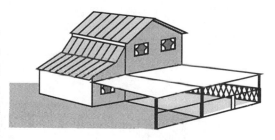

25

**Water Tank on Top**

Water tanks are normally concealed in the attic. By exposing it is like one who shows off his money in his pocket ending up losing it to a pickpocket. Likewise, by having the water tank on top

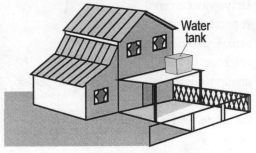

Water tank

of the porch fronting the main gate, one can expect one's wealth to flow away. The best solution is to remove the water tank to a neutral position in the house.

# 8. The Threshold of Fortune

The main gate area and the front of the house are important in feng shui. They form a threshold that either allow us to enter the outside world or to remain in our own comfortable zone of the shelter.

Besides allowing known friendly faces to enter our premises, the main gate area also allows us to prevent strangers from entering our property.

Thus this area which facilitates the interflow of forces from both ends must be cleared from obstacles that may influence the balance of feng shui. Other general pointers regarding our property are:

- A small house must not have a big front entrance because this is an imbalance and will cause disharmony;
- A house that sits on a higher ground with a sharp slope that leads towards the gate will have problems retaining the *chi*. Like water that finds its own level, *chi* is also found to flow outwards. it is not likely for such a house to have fortune;
- It is good to have trees if they are planted in the right area of a compound. But to have it planted near the front gate and to have them cast shadows will only bring bad luck to the owner.
- To have electrical wires which stretch from our front entrance to a terminal outside is to be a "nose-pulled front". This is considered unlucky to the owner, like an animal being pulled by the nose. The occupant will always find himself being

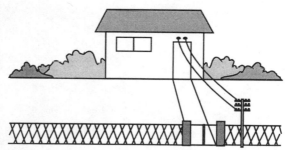

subjected to the control of other.

- To have a small horizontal drain in front of the house is to have a "take-off front". It only helps to drain off wealth from the occupant.

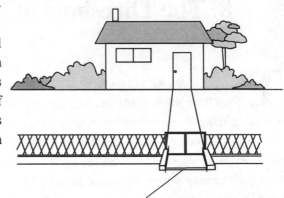

Small drain created here by owner of the house for easy drainage when it rains.

# 9. Types of Walls

**M**any house owners like to build boundary walls around their houses as it gives them a sense of security and a measure of privacy. These walls also help to cut down noise from the passing traffic and dust from the roadside. A word of caution though: these perimeter walls have a character of their own and a well-designed wall can enhance the feng shui of the house whilst a poorly-designed structure may bring adverse effects to the occupants.

### Conventional wall

A conventional wall with two prominent pillars on both sides of the gate, speaks of a well-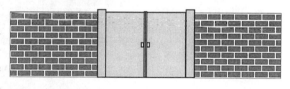balanced structure which augurs well for the feng shui of the house.

### Slanting Front

If the top edge of the wall slopes down towards the gate, it brings with it bad feng shui as 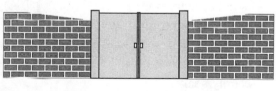wealth is said to drain away from the front.

### Slanting Sides

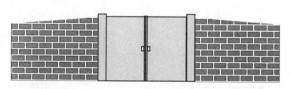A wall that slants down towards its side has bad feng shui as wealth can easily be lost in that direction.

29

## Tower Sides

A wall with strong prominent sides is reflective of a castle tower. It gives added

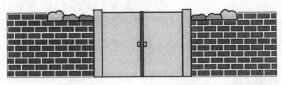

protection to the owner. However, to bring about a proper balance of *yin* and *yang* elements, have a row of plants at the lower edge to even up the wall.

## Negative Tower Sides

The small pillars flanking the gate at the far corners are out of balance when compared with the strong perimeters of the wall. The

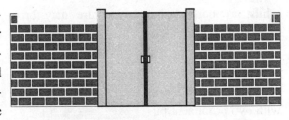

feng shui of the house is adversely affected, and would cause disharmony.

## The Smiling Wall

Like a mouth curved upwards, a boundary wall bearing this design reflects good vibes and

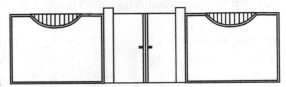

friendliness all round. Install a fence or metal grills where the open curve is, for security's sake.

## The Great Wall

Such a boundary wall is reminiscent of the Great Wall of China. It is a symbol of protection.

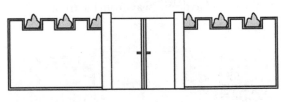

The gaps in between should be filled with plants to give the wall some life.

**Tomb Wall**

Tomb-shaped walls are for the dead, so they should not be used as a perimeter for the living.

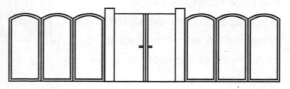

**Fiery Wall**

A wall with sharp edges piercing upwards is called the fire wall. As the fire element is often volatile and hard to control, to use it to surround

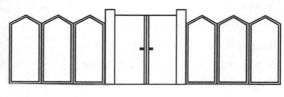

one's house is to place it in a ring of fire. So bitter quarrels are bound to break out in the family.

**Bamboo Wall**

Some perimeter walls are constructed in the shape of long bamboos. Hallow bamboos, ac-

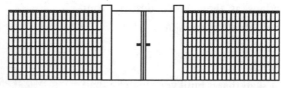

cording to popular belief, can send out pleasant sounds to bring life to all things on earth. Since man-made bamboo walls are anything but hollow, their effectiveness in bringing in good fortune is somewhat curtailed.

**Solitary Wall**

A solitary wall has upright pillars. Such a wall would create a sense of loneliness unless grills are placed in between the pillars.

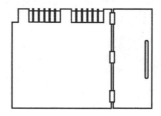

31

**Ancestor tablet**

A perimeter wall should not have the design of an ancestor tablet in remembrance of the dead. It is definitely bad feng shui to have surrounded one's house with such wall.

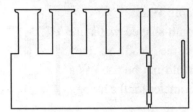

**Waves**

The top part of the wall has wave-like curves. Curved Walls symbolise a flow (of money) which eventually would be lost at the gate area.

**Jaws**

To keep a harmonious environment, your wall should not have sharp edges as they would destroy your neighbour's feng shui.

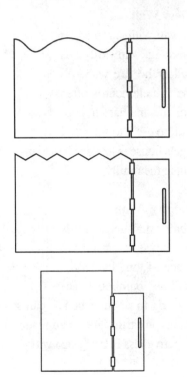

**Mega Wall**

A wall that is built very high has bad feng shui because it prevents *chi* from entering your home. Occupants would suffer bad health.

# 10. Ventilation Holes of Walls

**P**erimeter walls often serve to give some measure of privacy and security to the occupants of a house. This brick line of protection runs fine in feng shui if the walls are low with iron grilles fixed on the upper portion. The grilles will allow *chi* to flow freely into the compound and the house. However, there are instances where the brick walls are built much higher than the usual perimeter walls. This cuts off the flow of *chi* into the house, leaving an area full of stale *chi*. The health of the occupants will suffer as a result.

Some house owners build walls with ventilation holes to make up for the full-height solid walls. Let us take a look at the common shapes of these ventilation holes to see how they can affect the well-being of the occupants and the harmony of the house.

### Water Hole

A circle represents the water element. Round holes are not ideal shapes for ventilation holes for perimeter walls. As the circle symbolises the water element, and

water tends to find its own level, wealth is believed to flow out of the house.

### Square Hole

The square shape symbolises practicality and this down-to-earth design gives it a neutral characteristic.

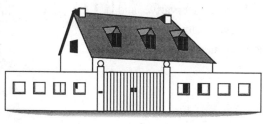

## Fire Hole

The triangle shape represents the fire element. A perimeter wall with triangles all round symbolises a house being surrounded by fire. The occupants of the house are likely to encounter lots of trouble whether in business or family life.

## Reverse Fire Hole

The reverse triangle is not a good shape to have either as it still symbolises the fire element. Even though the "fire" is "burning out", such a shape should be avoided.

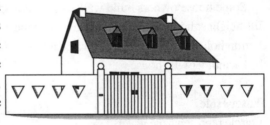

## Secretive Hole

Small vertical slits between the walls are known as secretive holes because of the narrow views offered. Such elements would reveal the conservative and secretive nature of the houseowner.

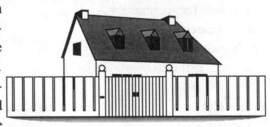

## The Arch

Like the arched doorways of imperial palaces in ancient China, such a pattern brings good feng shui. This is because when *chi* flows through these ventilation holes, the flat base which

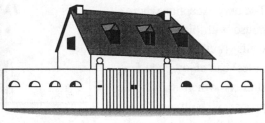

represents the earth element and the arched top which symbolises heaven, enable *chi* to spiral outwards in perfect harmony with the *yin* and *yang* elements.

## The Cup

The cup shape is actually an inverted arch. Though the notion of the cup is good, unfortunately the same does not hold true for a ventilation hole thus shaped. This is because the flat por-

tion, which is of the earth, cannot supersede the importance of heaven (the arch), by being on top of it.

## No Holes

A terrace house that is surrounded by a high brick perimeter wall without any ventilation holes in it has very bad feng shui. Since

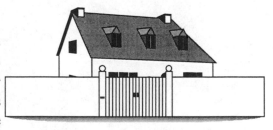

the flow of *chi* is cut off, stale *chi* builds up around the house and brings ill health and misfortune to the occupants.

## The Exception

The only exception where a house with high perimeter walls (but no ventilation holes) can enjoy good feng shui is when the house proper is built on higher ground than the surrounding wall. The solid wall then becomes just a small hurdle as *chi* can flow above the wall into the house to benefit the occupants.

## Pat Kua Holes

Due to its mystical nature, the *pat kua* ventilation hole is best used for walls around temples and places of worship.

# 11. Gates

To review the feng shui of a house, the geomancer would begin with the gate. This is because the gate is the first point which a person has to pass through in order to enter the premises.

Every member of the household has to use the gate, whether to the workplace, school or the market; as such, the gate is about the most used article of the house. Being the prime object that fronts the house, the gate should have a positive design so as to bring good vibes to the household. Here are samples of gate designs and their effects.

**Water Gate** (1)

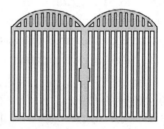

The water gate brings wealth if the path from the gate slopes inwards to the house. If it slopes outwards, one's wealth would flow away.

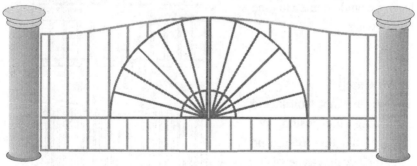

**Water Gate** (2)

A gate that is curved in design is called a watergate, and it has nothing to do with a former American president. Since the gate has a round design in the centre, a wheel motif is thus formed. As the wheel symbolises things going round and round, by using this gate, water (money) is made to flow.

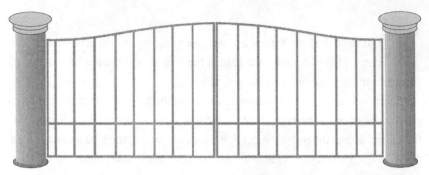

If the road leading from your gate slopes downwards, then you can expect your finances to go in that direction. But if the road from the gate to your house slopes inwards (towards your house), you can expect fortune to come in.

If you are uncomfortable with this water wheel gate, then have the wheel removed to cut down on the motion of the wheel churning away your wealth.

### Conventional Gate

This is a neutral design thus no harm would come to the houseowner.

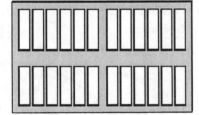

### Valley Gate

Valleys are not considered good feng shui position because of the flow of drastic *chi*, thus valley-type gates would bring negative results.

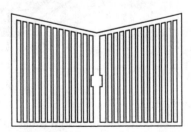

### 'Moderate' Fire Gate

The strength is at the peak, but because the symbol of the fire peaks moderately, it would not bring harm to the owner.

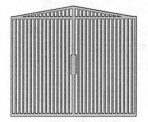

### Temperamental Gate

The V design goes in opposite directions. In feng shui, such ups and downs are not positive and cause a temperamental effect.

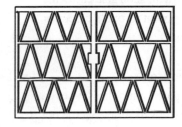

### X-gate

The X is a universal symbol that denotes the negative factor. Getting an X in your exam paper means you have failed. Trees marked with an X are tagged for felling. Crossroads are believed to be the devil's meeting point, thus, an X should not be used on a gate.

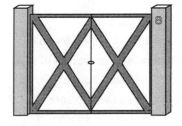

### Total Enclosed Gate

This gate would not allow *chi* to flow through freely, therefore it is deemed to be bad. Note that such gates are used by prisons, cutting off criminals from society.

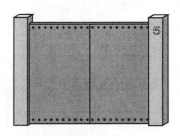

**Money Gate**

By using *chien* (money) motifs for the gate, one can hope to attract wealth.

**Gate of Growth**

The floral ornament, symbolises growth; such gate can bring development to one's career or business.

**Uneven Gate**

Such gate symbolises uneven nature, thus the home would not be harmonious.

**Down Trend Gate**

As the middle of the gate can help to determine the strength of the gate, a gate with design of bars going down in the centre bears negativeness as it shows one going on the down trend.

**Up Trend Gate**

Design of bars found in a gate which meet up in the centre of a gate is known as the 'up trend gate'. This kind of a gate carries positive elements as it leads one ambition towards the up trend.

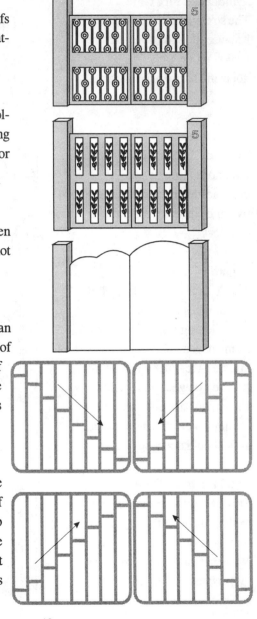

# 12. Gates of Convenience

**M**ost houses with big gates usually have a smaller gate so that one need not open the big gates for just one person entering or leaving the house. This smaller "gate of convenience" need not necessarily be part of the big gates; it can be beside the main gates. But whether it is built into the bigger gates, or on the sides, it qualifies as a "gate within a gate". Like two mouths that can be used to enter the house, the "gate within a gate" has to be properly positioned; a bad position would upset the good luck that flows into the house. (The following diagrams are viewed from outside the gates.)

### Dragon's domain

*Looking out from your house*, the left side of the gate is considered that of the Green Dragon. To position the "gate within a gate" there is to double the strength of the dragon positon. Good feng shui.

### Lower Left

This position although good feng shui, is not as good as the dragon's side. The reason is that the smaller gate is placed on the lower point of the gate, thus a weaker position.

### Independent Left
Good feng shui as the area left to the gate is also the area of the Green Dragon.

### Tiger's Lair
A "gate within a gate" on the right side is in an extremely negative position as this is the area of the White Tiger. The smaller gate in that position strengthens the Tiger, thus it dominates the Green Dragon. Bad feng shui.

### Lower Right
Also bad feng shui despite the smaller gate being in a weaker position on the tiger's side.

### Independent Right
This is still bad feng shui. A smaller gate on the far right from the main gate gives the White Tiger two "mouths" to overcome the Green Dragon.

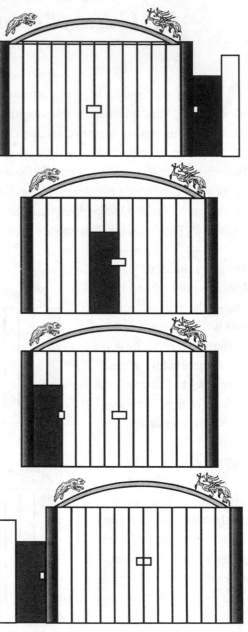

42

# 13. Letter-boxes

**A**ll of us could do with some good news to brighten up our lives. A free trip to some exotic destination, a prize won in a contest – we dream of the day when the postman will bring such great tidings in the mail.

More down-to-earth but not any less exciting is news of a successful shares application or an offer of a new job.

We may wonder then, why is it that some people have all the luck in the world, while others are not doing so well. In feng shui, the position of a letter-box determines to a large extent, the type of mail received. A letter-box that is placed at a vantage point will enhance the luck of the occupants of the house, while one that is poorly placed will adversely affect one's fortune.

It is interesting to note that the letter-box is painted red universally. Perhaps this is so because red is a vibrant colour that is said to bring good luck. (The diagrams below show the views from outside the gates.)

## Right Pillar with Rubbish Chute

This is not an ideal position for your letter-box because the rubbish chute below will mean that good luck coming your way will be countered by a streak of bad luck.

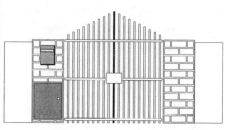

## Right Pillar

Most of us shake hands with our right hand; similarly, we receive gifts with that same hand. That being the case we should also place the letter-box at the right side of the gate.

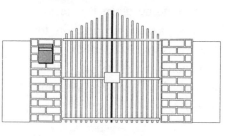

### Right Edge of Gate

The right-hand side at the edge of the gate is an excellent position for your letter-box. Good tidings will be ushered in whenever the gate is used.

### Centre of the Right Gate

This is a good position too, though it may not enjoy all the benefits that come with it being placed at the edge of the right side of the gate.

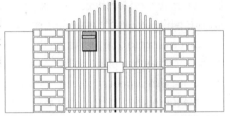

### Left Edge of Gate

Avoid placing your letter-box at the edge of the left side of the gate. Good luck will not find its way to your house.

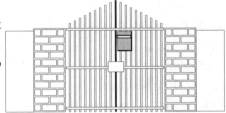

### Left Pillar

Another no-no when it comes to choosing a suitable position for your letter-box. A letter-box placed on the left pillar of the gate will not bring good tidings to the occupants of the house.

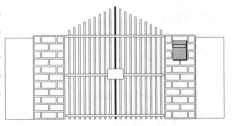

# 14. The Driveway

The driveway of a house is important as a conduit of *chi* from the main road to the house. If the linkage is well connected *chi* would have access into the house. If the linkage is badly connected *chi* is lost, interrupted or being disturbed along its way, the house would have a bad flow of *chi* coming in.

We look at some illustrations of driveways to understand its implication and the right steps to balance its woes.

## 1. Straight Driveway

A straight short driveway is normally found in terrace houses where the main gate faces the main door of the house. As it is best not to place a door which faces the main gate directly as *chi* tends to travel in too fast, a wind chime should be placed up on the house main door to slow the *chi* down.

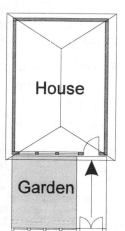

## 2. Driveway with Side Entrance

As all *chi* tends to travel in a straight line, a house that has one of its sides as an entrance should also have a mirror affixed on the wall (see illustration) to reflect the *chi* in.

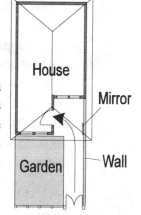

### 3. Driveway with Front Side Entrance

If the main door of a house does not end up to face a gate's pillar or a rubbish chute area and if the recess area that faces the main gate is not too deep, such a positioning is acceptable. However, if the recess area is found to be too deep, place lots of plants in that area to recycle *chi* so that the access of it would be pushed backwards to the house main entrance.

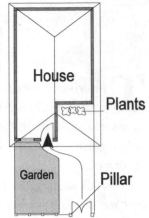

### 4. Driveway of a Semi-Detached Bungalow with a Side Entrance

If the main entrance of the semi-detached house is not being obstructed in anyway at its front, such driveway is acceptable.

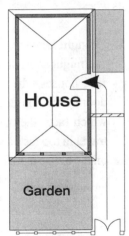

### 5. Driveway with Main Entrance at the Back

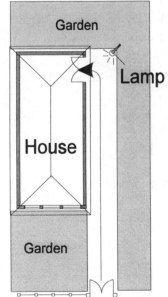

A main entrance of a house that is found at the far back of the house is not too good to have as *chi* has to travel past the whole house before it can really enter the house. To quicken the speed of *chi* to flow in to benefit the house, place a lighted lamp post to attract *chi* in.

# 15. Pillars

**P**illars are vertical columns that support heavy beams and structures. In feng shui, if a pillar in a building is placed at "unsuitable" positions, they can bring bad luck or problems to the dweller. Alternately, one can expect harmony when a pillar is well-positioned.

### Facing Door
A single pillar that faces the main entrance of a house brings bad luck as it blocks one's wealth.

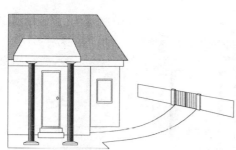

### Unbalanced Roof
If the positions of the columns are not symmetrical, resulting in one side of the roof that juts out being wider, such imbalance brings negative feng shui to the house.

### Higher-placed Inner Pillars
Having the inner pillars on higher ground is good feng shui, as it denotes a "high" status.

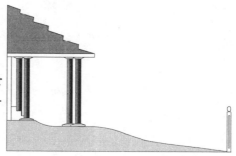

### Higher-placed Outer Pillars

Outer pillars that are on a higher level than the inner ones bring bad feng shui. They denote "demotion".

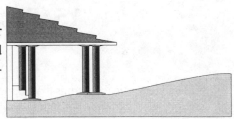

### Three Pillars

Even when the three pillars are evenly positioned and the number three (in Cantonese, *san*) has good connotation, the effect would still be negative when the central pillar blocks the door. Occupants would face obstacles in life.

### Good Position

Evenly placed pillars with the main entrance directly in between brings harmony and good fortune to the household.

# 16. Creating Pillars of Strength

T he phrase "pillar of strength" oozes with much positiveness. However, the location of a pillar ought to be viewed with caution. This is because a badly placed pillar can block the flow of *chi*. Let us look at the ways we can work around an ill-positioned pillar.

### Remove It

If the pillar is merely a decorative element, have it removed if possible.

Remove it

### Fine Flutes

Another solution would be to place bamboo flutes tied with red ribbons in the shape of *pat* (the figure eight in Cantonese, a number which denotes prosperity). This is a sure bet for siphoning off bad *chi*.

### Plant It There

Where it is not possible to remove the pillar, place a large potted plant next to it. As plants generate life force, and pillars are dead objects, the *chi* from the plant will help neutralise the negative forces of a pillar.

Bamboo flute with red ribbons

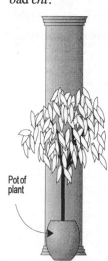

Pot of plant

## Mighty Mirror

As mirrors allow *chi* to penetrate through objects, install mirrors round the pillar to turn an adverse situation around.

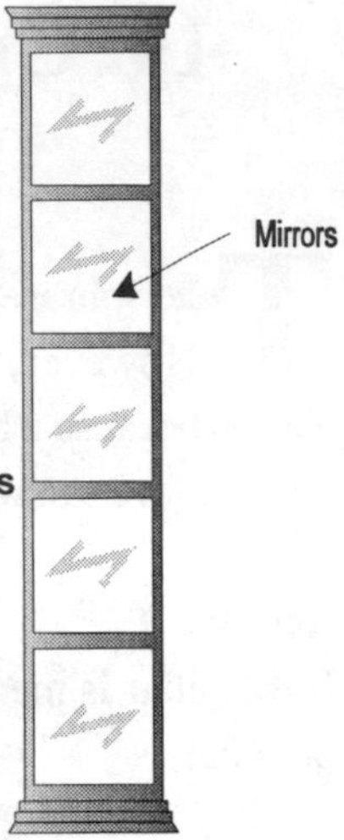

Mirrors

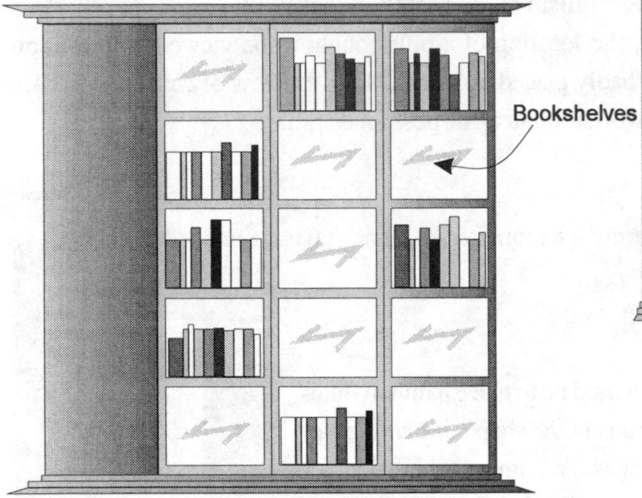

Bookshelves

## Shelf It

An innovative way of working around this problem in a house is to build cabinets or book shelves in such a way that the pillar becomes part of the structure.

# 17. Water - The Essence and Energy of Life

F licking through the pages of time, it is obvious that most civilisations began along rivers. Water has always been an essential element for life, more so when a civilisation is based on agriculture.

Living beside rivers, early man depended on the creatures in water as a source of protein and diverted water from streams into his land for crop cultivation.

Due to the properties of gravity and the propensity of water to seek its own level and thus creating a free flow of energy, rivers became liquid highways for early man.

Water, considered one of the softest substances in the world (as it can fit into any kind of container), is also strong because it can erode any hard substance given time.

The human body consists mainly of water. Through perspiration and other discharges, the body temperature remains constant. Loss of fluid has to be replaced in one form or another otherwise fatal dehydration can set in.

There is a saying which goes something like this: if something is earned with little effort, its value is often diminished. But when one loses it, its true worth is felt. This is true in respect of water — because we consume it daily, we take its importance for granted.

In Chinese, the word for water is *sui* which can also mean "money". This connection probably came about due to the importance water has always played in the life of man, ancient and modern.

A businessman can sometimes be heard to say that he is "rolling his money". If luck shadows his walk, he may roll it well to become wealthy and successful. But if his luck deserts him and his rolling gets seriously stuck, he may end up inviting creditors to his doorstep.

Good money can be said to be like running water that forever rolls and returns in plentiful supply. On the other hand, bankruptcy is like stagnant water that fails to give life.

In conclusion, to have water in our midst is to have life. Thus, whether one has more or less of it would depend on one's fate and how one balances one's feng shui.

# 18. The Way the Water Flows

T he Chinese have a way of saying "thai shui" (watch for water), which means to look out for the authorities. In feng shui, *thai shui* means being cautious about the way your wealth flows. As water symbolises wealth, it is believed that if one were to place a source of water in the right place, prosperity is assured.

## Outdoor Tap
Most houses have a garden tap to facilitate watering the garden or washing the car. It is best if the tap is placed facing the house so that prosperity would flow into the house.

## Exposed Roof Drain
To have an open roof drain is to have one's wealth fully exposed. Just like a poker player with his cards face-up on the table, a person in such a situation is at a disadvantage. To counter this, the drainage pipe should be extended towards the gutter so that water is not seen pouring out from the exposed pipe when it rains.

Joining the pipe to the roof gutter would prevent the water from being exposed.

Exposed drain pipe

**Water-closet**

To have a water-closet door facing the main door of the house is to lose money. Your can put a stop to such losses by either shifting the water-closet door or the house's main door.

**Basin**

Your wealth can also be siphoned out by a basin which faces the main door. The simplest way to rectify this is to change the door's position.

**Magnetic attraction**

Whether a house uses a square-tiled water container or an earthen jar for the bathroom, it is best that such a container be filled to the brim. This denotes abundance for the household.

# 19. The Drainage

**M**odern housing has drainage that carries away waste water from the premises. As water (*shui*) represents wealth, one should be careful how it flows, because a "good" drainage would enhance the feng shui of the house whereas a bad system would have adverse effects on the household.

### Side Escape
A drain that is outside the house with the outlet next to the main gate would make it hard for the house-owner to accumulate wealth.

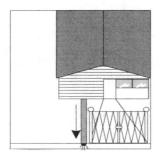

### Direct Escape
A direct drainage from the main door towards the gate. Difficult to accumulate wealth as water flows directly outwards.

### Exit next to Gate
Water travels inside the compound of the house before flowing out next to the main gate. This kind of drainage brings average fortune.

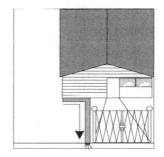

### Exit Away from Gate

Good drainage in feng shui. Water travels inside the compound and makes its way out through an outlet away from the main gate.

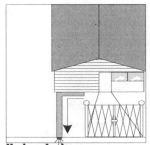

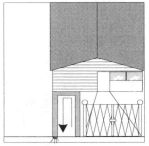

### Quarter Fortune

Water circulates only a quarter of the compound before being discharged. The house-owner would only receive a quarter his fortune.

### Full circulation

Good drainage in feng shui. Water circulates the compound before being discharged.

- Normally these types of circulation are found in bungalows.

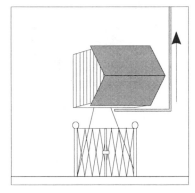

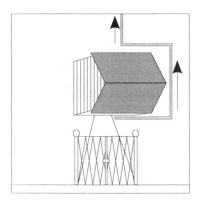

### Half Fortune

As the drain surrounds half the compound of the house, half of the fortune goes to the house-owner.

## Three-quarter Fortune

Good feng shui as drainage surrounds almost the house completely.

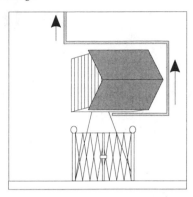

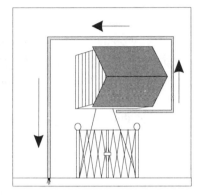

## Full Circle

Excellent feng shui as water flows around the house ensuring that wealth goes around every corner.

## Twin Dragon Flow

This bungalow has a "twin dragon flow". Again, feng shui is excellent for one who lives in such a house.

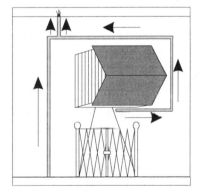

# 20. The Door

**D**oors provide entrances to buildings and since they act as a threshold from one room to another, they are also believed to be entrances to other worlds.

There is a saying that if you want to see a ghost, the doorway is the ideal place to start with. Standing there as it is, the door would be half open, and if you peer past its edge long enough, you might just see some spirits. Should you want to end your little adventure, just slam the door hard – that should disperse the spirits.

It has also been said that if you have this nasty habit of opening doors and never closing them, you will probably end up never owning a house. Whatever we believe in or choose not to believe in, doors are exciting where feng shui is concerned.

Doors are very important in feng shui. A well-placed door is said to bring in good luck, while a badly-placed door can leak out *chi* and energy from the house. Let us look at some badly placed doors, and what we can do to bring harmony to the house.

### Main Door which Opens Outwards

The front door is said to welcome in good fortune, so a door which opens outwards is undesirable as all the luck will fall out. **Remedy**: Have the door open inwards so that the luck will flow in.

### An eye-to-eye door

This is a door which has a knob directly facing another door knob. Such a door tends to breed insincerity among the members in the house-

58

hold, as nobody wants to see another in the proper light. **Remedy**: Have the middle part of the knob painted in red to create "life and fire" in the eye of the knob. This will encourage members to view each other in the proper perspective.

## Overlapping Doors

Such doors are considered unlucky because it symbolises the act of slapping each other's face. Domestic quarrels and fights are likely in such households. **Remedy**: Hang a long scroll or painting on the empty wall next to the door to create balance and harmony at home.

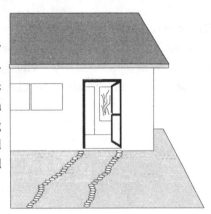

## Door-face-door

This is a door which faces another door. As *chi* travels swiftly in a straight line, the occupant will find it hard to accumulate wealth. **Remedy**: The best solution is to realign the inner door away from the main door. It this is not possible, hang a wind chime at the top of the main door to break the forceful flow of incoming *chi*.

## Staircase which faces the Main Door

Such an arrangement is said to drag the occupant's luck down. **Remedy**: Realign the staircase by curving it away from the front door.

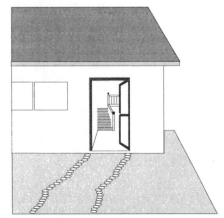

**Back door which invites bad *chi* in**

Most rubbish and refuse are found at the back of a house. So a back door which open inwards is said to invite bad *chi* in. **Remedy**: Have the back door open outwards so that unwanted *chi* can be directed out of the house.

**A hole in the front**

A window directly facing the main door is considered bad *chi* because incoming chi is being siphoned away. **Remedy**: Place a tall potted plant between the door and the window to prevent total loss of fortune.

# 21. Types of Door

L et us look at the front doors of houses and their effects on the household.

**Single Wooden Door**
Good feng shui. A wooden door of a standard size that opens inwards generally brings good fortune.

**Glass Door**
Negative feng shui. *Chi* easily penetrates a transparent door. This type of door exposes one's strength, and no household secret can be kept from friends and neighbours.

**Sliding Glass Door**
Negative feng shui. A three-piece door allows even more *chi* to pass through. "Easy come, Easy go", so the owner would hardly have savings.

**Double door**

Negative feng shui. A small terrace house should not have a double door because it would be out of proportion with the building.

**Half-Glass Door**

Negative feng shui. Typical of an office door, this type of door is sometimes called the *yang* door because activities associated with the door take place between 9 am and 5 pm. A house is where the family finds rest and peace of mind, therefore this type of door should not be used.

**Revolving Door**

Negative feng shui. This type of door is used in hotels, casinos and restaurants to "gobble up" business. Therefore one should not use it for the house if one does not want to be "swallowed" by his own home.

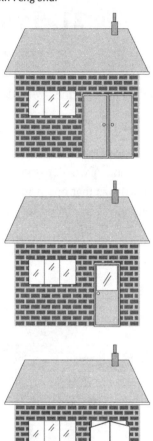

**Metal Door**

Negative feng shui. Never use a metal door for a house. As the metal element is cold, one would find it hard to make friends.

# 22. The Block to Success

Most of us often take a good look from our house to see if there are any obstacles in the surroundings which disrupt the feng shui of our house. Whether it is in the form of a tree, a sign post or a small hill, a *pat kua* would come in handy in deflecting *sha chi* (negative energy). However, there are times when the obstacle lies within our very own compound, and not outside the perimeters of our garden. Such an obstacle can be very serious and damaging to our well-being because it affects us without our knowing it. This is called fatal block or point blank blocking. A common illustration of fatal blocking is when the main entrance of a house ends up confronting a solid blank wall or a pillar.

For example, if the object is a solid wall, whenever an occupant opens the door to leave the house, he would run into a fatal block. And assuming that he uses the main door five times a day in a week, he would have a total of 35 confrontations with the wall. In a year, he would have literally knocked into the wall 1,820 times. Whether it is a blank wall or a pillar, if the confrontation is frequent enough, subconsciously his psyche would be affected. The end result would be the actualisation of problems which he would have to face daily.

Let us take a look at some of the common blockings that often go unnoticed and how best to overcome it.

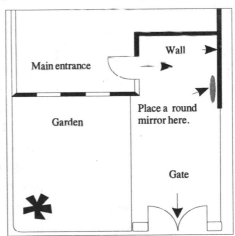

## Confronting Wall
The main door opens to face a wall that runs parallel to the house. This problem can be easily overcome by hanging a round or oval mirror on the wall.

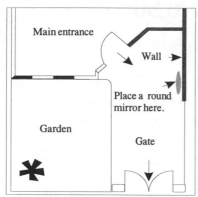

## At An Angle

Even though the main entrance of this house is at an angle, it still opens to face a solid wall, thus running into a fatal blocking. Just as in the earlier example, a round or oval mirror placed on the wall would take care of the situation.

## Confronting Pillar

Two pillars located just outside the entrance may create an aesthetic look. But due to the closeness to the main door, and the fact that you have to walk towards the pillar whenever you leave the house, a fatal confrontation is seen here. You can easily get around this problem by placing a pot of tall plant to cushion off the ill effects of the confrontation.

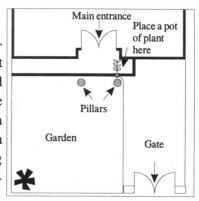

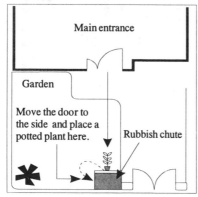

## Confronting Rubbish Chute

If your problem is one of facing the rubbish chute, for a start you can move the door of the rubbish chute to the side so that it does not face your main door directly. At the same time, place a potted plant next to where the door of the rubbish chute used to be.

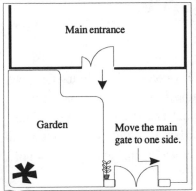

Main entrance

Garden

Move the main
gate to one side.

### Confronting Gate Pillar

When the main door is badly located, it may end up having a fatal confrontation with the gate pillar. In that case, you should move the gate to another side. If that is not possible, place a big pot of plant next to the gate pillar.

# 23. Iron Grilles

I ron grilles are a common sight in many homes. Considering that petty thefts and burglaries are quite rampant in some neighbourhoods, perhaps such preventive measures are understandable. A house without grilles might seem like an open invitation to burglars, and its occupants would not be able to enjoy a sense of security. When looking at the feng shui of a house, grilles do play an important role too.

## The Prison

Such designs are often found in houses of the pre-war era. Because the vertical bars on the window bear a close resemblance to that of a prison cell, the occupants of such homes can easily run foul of the law.

## The Net Grille

The net grille has a negative effect on the feng shui of a house. The net symbolises a snare or trap, and the occupants are likely to find themselves trapped in their own situation and unable to make much progress in life.

## Reverse Fortune Grille

The reverse fortune grille which dips downward suggests that the occupants of the house would share a similar downward trend in their career.

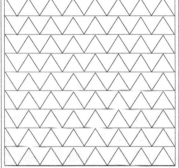

## The Achiever's Grille

This has just the opposite effect of the reverse fortune grill as the arrow-like design spells success and promotion for the occupants. Suited for the ambitious who look forward to a career boost.

**The Triangular Grille** This one is also considered to be representative of the fire element. The symbol itself depicts instability.

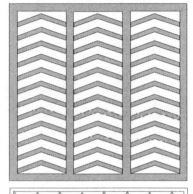

## The Diamond Grille

Diamonds may be a girl's best friend but when it comes to window grilles, the symbol itself also depicts the fire element. To have this element displayed so prominently in one's house is to have lots of arguments and quarrels.

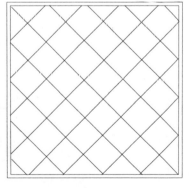

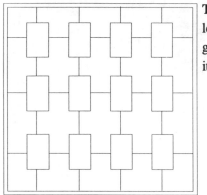

**The Rectangular Grille** Like the four legs of a chair, rectangular and square grilles denote the same thing – stability.

**The Chien Grille** The chien grille itself symbolises money. To have it in one's house is to attract wealth into the home.

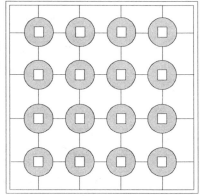

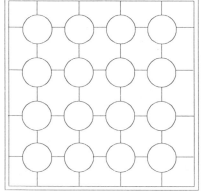

**The Round Grille** A round grille would enhance the occupants of the home, so that they can be more sociable and well-rounded in life. This sort of grille would be good for diplomats, PR people, sales executives and businessmen.

# 24. The Altar

**P**ious people have altars at home, where daily prayers are performed to seek blessings from the divine. The altar can also be regarded as a spiritual sentry that protects the house from forces of evil. In order for an altar to be effective, it has to be placed at proper positions.

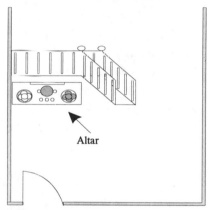

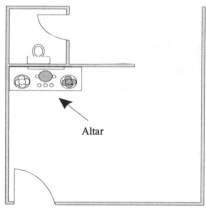

### Sacrilege

Having the altar beneath the staircase is no good because it should not be in a position where a man walks over it.

### Toilet Backing

Even if the altar faces the right direction, having it backed up by a toilet would bring bad luck instead.

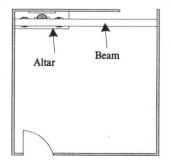

### Weighed Down

An altar under a beam would be in a "pressured" position thus it is better to move it elsewhere to maintain harmony at home.

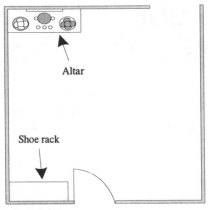

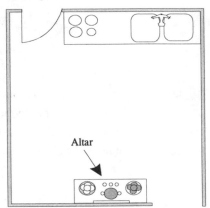

## Seeing Shoes

Avoid having a shoe rack that faces the altar as such a move would denote ill respect.

## In the Kitchen

Unless it is the altar that honours the Kitchen God, the main altar should not be placed in the kitchen because the smoke and oil would cloud the altar.

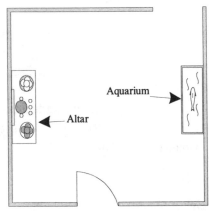

## Facing Water

As an altar is a place for offerings, incense is often burned on it. As such, water elements like an aquarium or sink should not be placed opposite it as this would extinguish one's offerings.

## In the bedroom

The family altar should never be placed in a bedroom as any act of intimacy would defile the sanctity of the altar.

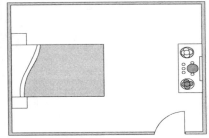

## Facing Room Door

Petitions made at the altar are supposed to be taken up to heaven. So it is a bad idea to have an altar facing the bedroom door as one's life force will also be dragged upwards, causing one to lose *chi* unnecessarily.

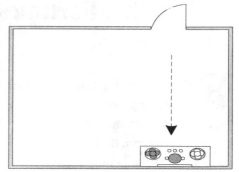

## Good Positions

The rule of thumb is that an altar should have a solid wall behind it for support. Secondly, it should occupy a vantage point that commands over all who enter the house.

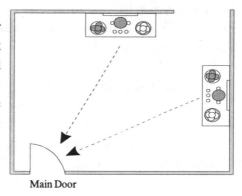

Main Door

# 25. Fortune Corners

**F**ortune corners are lucky corners which may be found in a house or business premises. They are usually located near the entrance. Good fortune corners are corners which are strategically located so that pristine *chi* coming in is trapped there for a moment before it is allowed to spiral away to other parts of the house. These corners are considered powerful corners because they trap the first breath of life taken in by the house. As the first breath of life has generative properties and creative forces, placing lucky items here would enhance one's fortune.

## 1. Doors in Straight Line

A house with doors running in a straight line usually does not have any fortune corner as the swift *chi* coming in heads straight out of the last door.

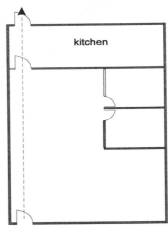

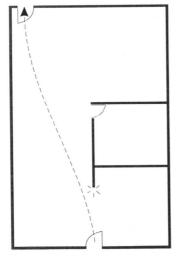

## 2. Protruding Wall

A protruding wall facing the main door splits *chi* as soon as it enters the house. Thus any good luck that heads your way is likely to be destroyed.

### 3. Lost in Toilet

It is bad feng shui to have your main door facing the toilet door as your fortune will go down the drain too. No fortune corner will be found in such a house.

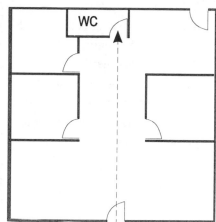

### 4. Underneath Staircase

This house could have found its lucky corner underneath a staircase, if there was a wall or something solid by the side of the staircase to break the flow of *chi* coming in. Unfortunately, such is not the case. Another factor that does not work in its favour is the fact that the movements of the occupants up and down the staircase will disrupt any luck coming in.

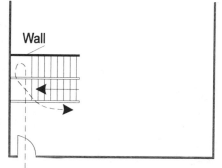

### 5. Store

It is no good to have the storeroom facing the mian door of the house as its fortune corner is found inside there. Thus, *chi* would be stagnant there and so is one's luck.

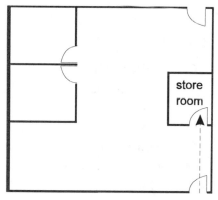

### 6. Too Far

This fortune corner is found right at the end of a house. In this manner it is called the 'Too-Far-Fortune-Corner'. As such, such corners are not deemed lucky as luck passes through the whole house before one could receive any.

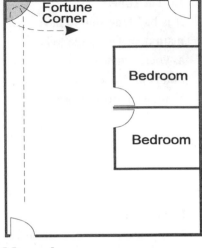

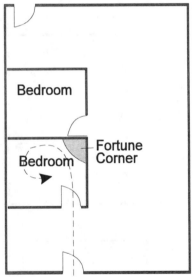

### 7. Monopoly

As the front bedroom is in line towards the house main door, *chi* that rushes in would enter this room first enhancing this room's corner. As such this particular room monopolises the house good luck leaving the rest of the occupants miserable.

### 8. Cannot Hold Corner

A short wall that juts out in line where *chi* enters a house would find it hard to hold this 'life force' is known as the 'Cannot Hold Corner'. It does not bring much positiveness to the occupants of this house.

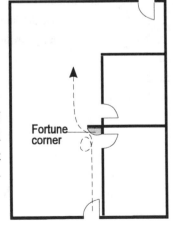

## 9. First in Line

This house certainly has a fortune corner, however, as the door of the first room lies in the direction where the *chi* would next disperse, this room would be the luckiest followed by others which would be less lucky.

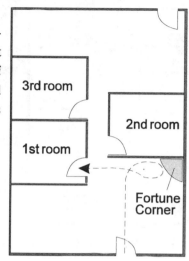

## 10. Cutting Edge Corner

A corner with too many edges is not a perfect corner. It is not too good for a house to have such corner as it cuts up one's luck.

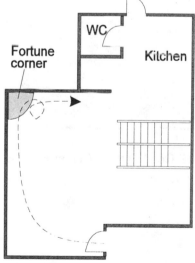

**11.** Good Fortune Corner is found here

75

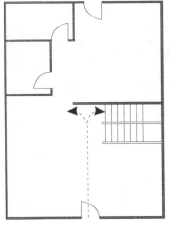

### 12. Diverted by Staircase

Direct *chi* coming into this house is diverted by a staircase wall which split *chi* into two directions. Thus this kind of setting is not too positive.

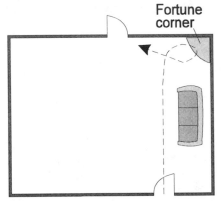

13. Good Fortune Corner is found here.

14. Good Fortune Corner is found here.

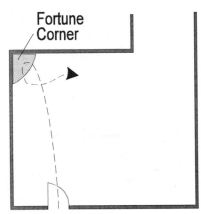

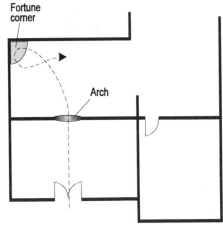

15. Good Fortune Corner is found here.

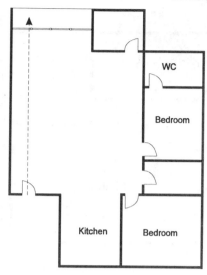

**16. Lost Through Balcony** (Negative)
An apartment door that opens inwards to face directly a balcony door would have no fortune corners as *chi* that flows in is totally lost straight out through the balcony door. Thus creating no fortune corner.

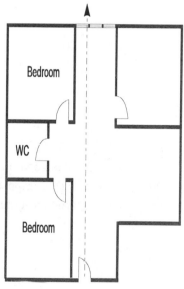

**17. Entrance Facing Window** (Negative)
An entrance door that faces a window of an apartment also loses *chi* out directly, thus creating no fortune corner for the occupants.

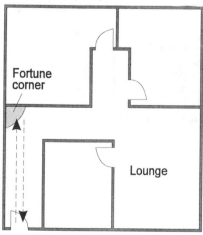

**18. Entrance Door Facing Corner** (Negative)
A fortune corner that faces a door directly does receive direct *chi* which in turn loses its energy back towards the same door. Such a corner has negative inclination as luck cannot be held.

### 19. Entrance Door Faces Bedroom Door

Similar to the above, *chi* that found its way into this bedroom also find its way back towards the main door, thus it is lost.

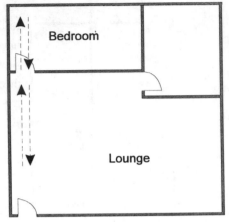

### 20. Good Fortune Corner (Positive)

This illustration has good fortune corner as *chi* is trapped and circulated around at this point.

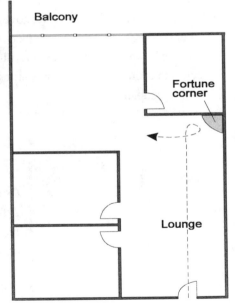

# 26. The Lucky Items

After having identify the fortune corners, we should place lucky items there to enhance our luck. Otherwise even if you have a lucky corner, it would be a waste if luck is not utilised fully. We will look at some examples of lucky items which you may want to place at your special corner.

**Conch Shell**
It is believed that conch shell can pro-duce a beautiful sound like Buddha's speaking. Its symbol also brings good fortune.

**Fortune Pot**
Like a magnet, a glass pot or jar filled up to the very top with money, would help to attract in more money.

**Money Plant** *Scindapsus aureus*
Naturally one can also place a pot of money plant at the fortune corner to attract in more money. How-ever, make sure that your money plant always stay alive and healthy.

**Maneki-Neko**
Probably the most widely acknowledged good luck cat in Japan is the Maneki-Neko. People love to have them as mascots to bring in happiness and fortune.

## Counting Fortune

One can also hang up an abacus and place a piggy bank below the abacus. This would symbolise one forever counting money and having a place for money to be stored up. However, make sure that your piggy bank is filled up with some money!

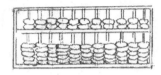

## The Genie

A ceramic genie is also a good symbol to be placed in a fortune corner as it symbolises the granting of one's wishes.

## The 3-Legged Toad

The 3-legged toad with a wide mouth biting a coin symbolises that money would be brought in.

## The Lucky Buddha

Like Santa Claus, the Lucky Buddha carries a big bag behind its back. The bag is supposed to contain the many treasures that one dreams of.

## The Fatty Buddha

Its prominence lies in its fat, protruding stomach which the Chinese believe to be a symbol of prosperity. It is believed that if one rubs the stomach each morning before going to work the person would have good luck.

## Hotei
The famed Oriental God Hotei with raised arms, is a
God of Fortune.

### Prag Nan Kwak
A kneeling Thai deity
with her right hand "calling in" business and her
left hand carrying a container which is used for
storing up her wealth. This is popularly found in
the homes of many Thais.

### Fook, Luk, Sau
The Chinese most famous trinity of Fook, Luk and Sau when placed in a
house is believe to bring longevity, luck and prosperity.

# 27. The Staircase

**A** double storey house often has a staircase. If such connection is well-positioned, good harmony would follow. However, if a staircase is badly positioned, obstructing or channelling too much *chi* away, the owner will suffer from the loss of luck and fortune.

A staircase that meets the front entrance of a house is considered to have bad feng shui because too much *chi* is drawn away from it. When too much energy is found to be siphoned off, fortune and luck are also believed to be lost in such a manner.

If the staircase is built away from the entrance of the house, half the portion of the staircase would be obstructing the flow of *chi* into the house. Because of such positioning much of the owner's opportunity would be blocked off.

Back

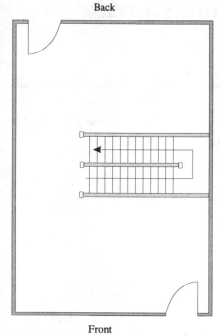

Front

An executing staircase is normally found in a compact double storey house whereby such staircases are placed right in the centre of the house leaving only two to three feet for passage. Because of such positioning, the house is cut into two. In such cases, whatever the owner does, his work and business would also be halved.

A spiral staircase that is found in the middle of a house is considered as bad feng shui because its position and shape would channel and thrust *chi* too violently upwards causing great upheaval in the family.

Unlike many shop lots that have two staircases, one in the front and the other at the back as a fire escape, a house or building that has only one staircase that faces the back door is considered as bad feng shui. The reason is because the back of a house is where rubbish is left for the garbage men, and if the staircase faces the back door bad and smelly *sha chi* is invited to enter the upper floor.

# 28. Beneath the Staircase

**O**ne would usually find items such as newspapers, mops, brooms and odds and ends stacked up beneath the staircase of one's house. But the space beneath the staircase need not be an eyesore. We can put it to good use to enhance the feng shui of the house.

### The Store

A nice little store can be created below the staircase to put away your shoes, brooms and other unsightly objects. Walled up, the exterior of the store presents an elegant front which is good for feng shui.

### The Support

If there is an air-well adjacent to a staircase, it might be a good idea to knock down the lower portion of the wall that separates the space beneath the staircase from the air-well. In that way, an indoor garden can be created. As plants are lower life forms, they symbolise support for the staircase. This serves to strengthen relationships between the occupants on the first floor and the ground floor.

Air-well

## Control of Wealth

Given the above scenario, you can go
one step further and build a small
pond with waterfall if space permits.
As water (*shui* in Cantonese) means
wealth, clever use of the space below
the staircase will ensure that you have
control over the flow of wealth and
are able to stay on top of things.

## Sacrilege

Never place an altar underneath a
staircase. Whenever you walk up the
stairs, your feet would be "stepping"
on the altar. That would be sacrile-
gious and bad fortune might befall the
occupants of the house.

## Mini Bar

In some houses you might find a mini
bar tucked away in the little corner
under the stairs. That might not be
such a nifty idea, considering that
someone will be walking up and
down the stairs and *chi* would be
pressing down on you who are serv-
ing drinks to guests. This would put
you at a disadvantage as a host/host-
ess.

# 29. The Staircase Connection

L ike *yin* and *yang*, the lower and upper levels of a house have to be properly connected by the staircase to ensure good feng shui to the occupants. If the connection is improper, it would upset the balance of feng shui of the house.

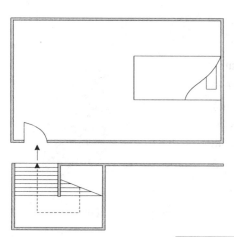

**Facing Bedroom**

The *chi* would mostly flow into the bedroom, resulting in unequal distribution of *chi* to the upper floor. On the other hand, the luck of the occupant of this room would be "flowing" down the stairway.

**Protruding Banister**

Banisters that point to the bedroom door is like a pin sticking out, thereby causing problems to the occupant of the room.

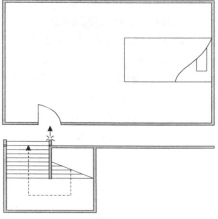

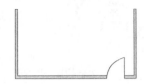

## Facing Pillar

The pillar would end up blocking the *chi* flowing up from the ground floor.

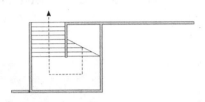

## Facing Toilet

Luck that comes up from the staircase ends up being flushed away. It does not matter whether you keep the toilet door open or closed. Your luck would still be flushed away as a door is still a door. Since it is impossible to relocate the staircase, the next best thing is to move the toilet door to the room that share a common wall with the toilet.

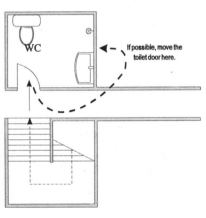

## Facing Store-room

All the *chi* would end up being stored there, thereby not bene-fiting the occupants of the house.

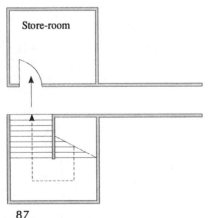

87

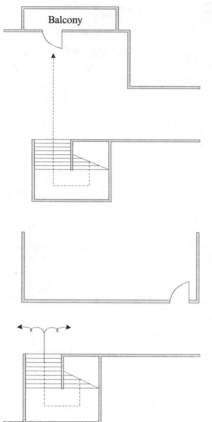

### Facing balcony

All the luck that comes up would end up flowing out from the balcony.

### Facing Wall

Having a wall where the staircase meet with the upper floor is good feng shui because *chi* ends up being dissipated to other parts of the area.

# 30. Crushed by Demons
# (Bei Quai Chaak)

hen night falls, many people would seek a peaceful and good
night's sleep. Subconsciously, our minds may be transported to
some dreamland where reality is often distorted by fantasy. But there are
some people who dread going to sleep because they fear recurring
nightmares. Perhaps the most fearful experience that we could have is *bei
quai chaak* or being crushed by a ghost. In the West, this repulsive
experience is called the Old Hag attack.

In Old English, this is called *nicht mara* (*mara* means "crusher" with
similar forms occurring in other Germanic language). Filipinos call this *ban-
gungut*, Tagalog for "nightmare". In Latin, the word *inuus* (one who sits on)
is used. In Greek, it is called *nigalion* (throttlers).

An example of *bei quai chaak* is described by Finley Hurley. He recalls:
"I was convinced that I would die within seconds if I didn't manage to move,
however slightly, to break the paralysis that gripped me. Instantly awakened
from a deep sleep, I could not move or cry out as I felt something draining the

life from my chest. I succeeded, after moments of intense and silent struggle, in opening my eyes and breaking the paralysis. And as my eyes opened, I thought I saw a black cloud swiftly recede from my bed."

Victims of *bei quai chaak* state that they experience a sense of wakefulness and fearfulness, and suffer from paralysis of their entire bodies. They may even sense a pressure on the chest followed by a sudden fear of death. Sometimes they hear footsteps approaching the bed.

David J. Hufford, a behavioural scientist and folklorist, at first surmised that these experiences happen only in Asia because of the deep-rooted superstition of the people. However, he later concluded that in both Newfoundland and the United States, one in every five person had experience *bei quai chaak*.

Whatever the thing that comes to disturb some unfortunate people during their sleep, imaginary, real or psychological, one thing is certain: this kind of experience is sometimes lethal. To dispel unwanted intruders in our mindscape, the Chinese believed that how and where the bed is placed is important.

# 31. Positioning of Bed

**I**s your bed placed in the best position in the bedroom? In feng shui, the key to having a good night's rest is in the positioning of beds. If the bed is placed in the right spot, you can be assured of a good night's sleep. There are also positions that your should avoid.

### Facing the Door
If you sleep with your head facing the bedroom door, your vitality will be drained away. Sleeping in this direction also allows spirits to roam into the room and you are likely to have nightmares or *bei quai chaak* (crushed by the demon).

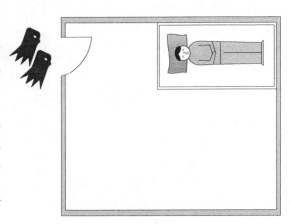

### Coffin Position
Sleeping with your legs facing the door is commonly known as the "coffin position" because it is the same position in which a deceased person is placed in his house before the funeral.

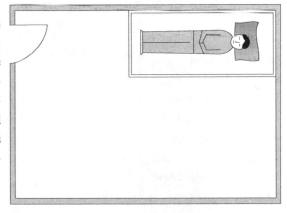

**Behind the door**

To sleep behind or too close the bedroom door will cause restlessness, because a door is often used.

**Low Point**

It is bad luck for someone to sleep with his head facing another person's feet. In certain countries in the olden days, people paid respect to royalty by kissing their king's feet. This denoted that the subject was of a lower status. When one sleeps in this manner, one would find it impossible to rise up the ladder of success.

**Facing the Toilet**

The toilet is a place where waste is disposed of. To sleep facing toilet would bring misfortune as the bad vibes from that direction will cause sickness.

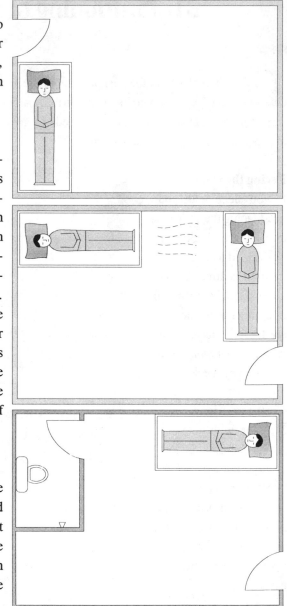

## Light Above

Never have a strong light directly over your head. The direct glare will spoil your eyes. In acupuncture, the eyes' source of energy is from the liver and gall bladder. These two organs will be affected when your eyes are affected.

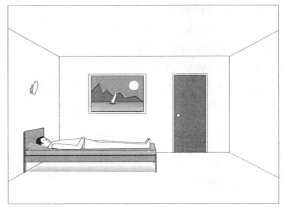

## Effects of Metal Bed

A metal bed is harmful because it allows *yin chi* from the ground to creep into one's body. You will end up with chronic ailments.

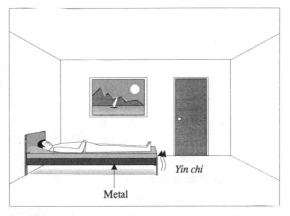

*Yin chi*

Metal

## Restful Night

Always place your bed parallel to the floorboards, otherwise *chi* running along the floorboards will cut across your sleeping position and cause insomnia.

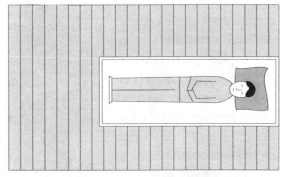

93

## Facing the Mirror

A mirror should not face the foot of your bed. This is because you may be frightened by your own image should you wake up and catch sight of your reflection. This can cause shock, nervousness or even heart attack.

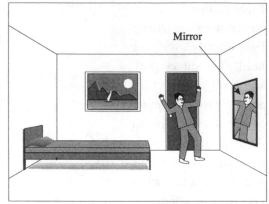

## Bed on Wheels

A bed with rollers is not good because it symbolises restless sleep. It also reminds one of hospitals where such beds are commonly found.

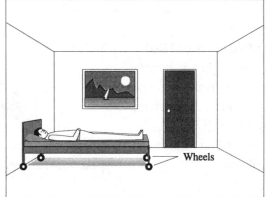

## Bed placed at an angle

Even though your horoscope may say that you should sleep in a certain direction, and that may mean that you may have to place your bed at an angle. But your bed should never be placed at an angle because all angles trap *chi*, and the enormous energy accumulated could disorientate you or disturb your peace of mind.

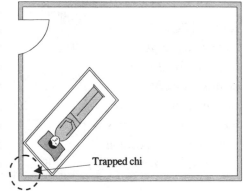

## Sleeping on the Floor

Sleeping on the floor without a proper bed is bad feng shui because the earth has lots of *yin chi*, and the human body can easily absorb this energy. In the long run, over-accumulation of such elements may lead to rheumatism or liver disorder.

## Below Three Feet is Best

The height of a bed should not be over three feet, otherwise accidents could befall the person.

## Above Knowledge Position

It is bad practice to keep books or any form of literature under your bed. Sleeping on top of such materials is regarded as disrespect for knowledge. Such a sleeping position would not benefit anyone who is seeking any form of academic knowledge.

## Mountain Position

It is good feng shui to sleep with your headboard firmly placed against the wall. The wall is symbolic of a mountain backing one's repose and could do you a lot of good.

## Concrete Slab

A concrete slab above one's bed brings pressure on one's sleeping position. The solution is to position your bed elsewhere in the room away from the slab.

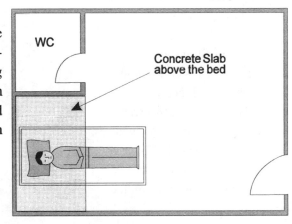

## At Lower Level

A bedroom may consist of two floor levels. A person's relationship with others will be eroded if he sleeps on a bed which is placed at the lower level. Furthermore, a wedding photo should not be placed facing the door as this is akin to a marriage being shown the exit. The best way out in this situation is to trade this bedroom with another in the house.

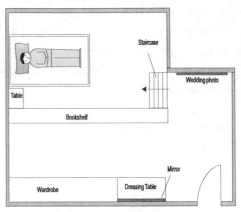

## Between Two High Cupboards

It is bad feng shui to have a bed sandwiched between two high cupboards as these could block the flow of *chi* and depriving you of having fresh *chi* (life force). It is advisable to remove one of the cupboards.

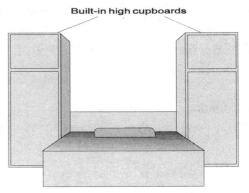

## Towards the Stairway

A bedroom that is closest to the staircase should not have the head of the bed position towards the stairway. It you do so, your life will be 'downhill'. For better harmony, relocate your bed in a position away from the stairway.

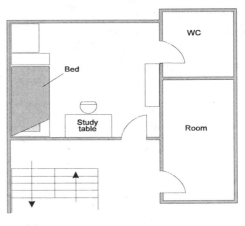

## In Line with Toilet

Placing the head of the bed next to the toilet wall is bad feng shui as moisture from the toilet would seep through the wall to affect one's health. The same applies if one side of the bed is aligned to the toilet. It one can shift the bed to the centre of the room as shown in the diagram, it would be fine.

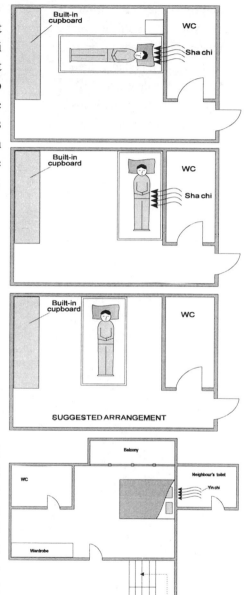

## Neighbour's Toilet

If the headboard is placed against the common wall that you are sharing with your neighbour, you should try to find out what is located behind the wall. If a toilet happens to be there, knowing the negative implication, we should move our bed away from that direction.

**Backed by Wooden Partition**

Check your partition to see whether it shakes easily or is firmly set up. It it is shaky, then your artificial wall is not ideal. But if it is firm, then one is assured of a good back-up.

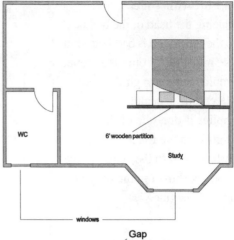

**No Backing**

Do not leave a gap between your bed and the wall as it signifies a lack of support. Thus the best is to push the head of the bed to touch against the wall to give it a solid backing.

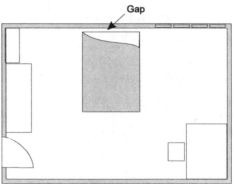

98

# 32. Positioning Mirror in Bedroom

**T**here is much controversy over the placing of mirrors in bedrooms. Some people believe that mirrors should not be placed directly facing the bed, while others see nothing wrong with that. So who do we believe?

To have a better understanding of the role of mirrors in feng shui, one should always bear in mind that a mirror has the power to attract one's image. As such, it can also attract one's soul which is believed to float a couple of feet above the body when we sleep. So if a mirror is badly positioned in the bedroom, it can reflect the soul out through the door. When this happens, your sleep will be disturbed or you might find yourself having out-of-body experiences or nightmares. Some feel themselves falling from high places. Others may feel exhausted upon waking up, even though they have slept for long hours, or they may wake up in cold sweat.

Here we examine the different positions in which mirrors can affect a person, in relation to the bedroom door. The black spots marked on the diagram indicate the best place to reposition the mirror to restore harmony in the room.

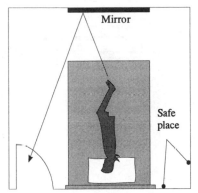

**Bed directly facing a mirror**

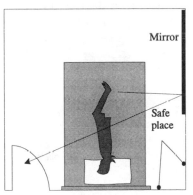

**Mirror facing one's right at the foot of the bed**

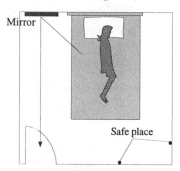

**Mirror facing one's left**

**Mirror facing one's right**

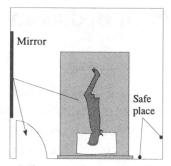

**Mirror directly facing the entrance near the right of one's head**

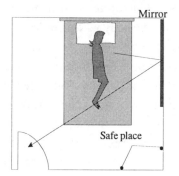

**Mirror facing one's left**

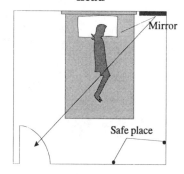

**Mirror on the left of one's head**

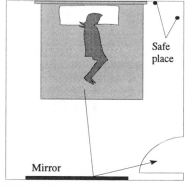

**Mirror directly facing one's self**

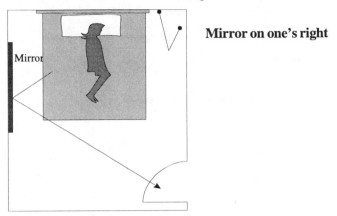

**Mirror on one's right**

**The best place to put the mirror**

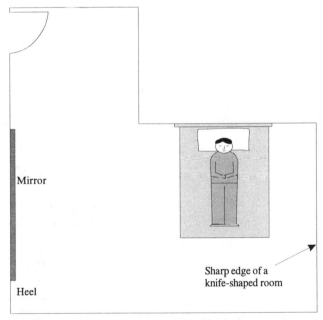

In a shoe-shaped room, it is best not to place one's bed at its heel or the front area, otherwise one would be stepped on or kicked about.

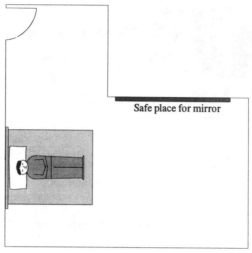

Safe place for mirror

A bed placed away from the heel and front of the foot of the shoe-shaped bedroom is ideal for a good rest.

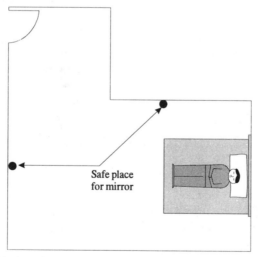

Safe place
for mirror

If your bed is in a shoe-shaped room, place a high mirror on the suggested spots to attract one's image from that position.

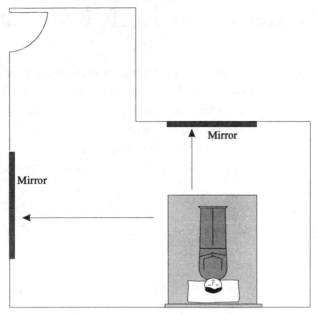

In a step down position, you can balance the negativeness by putting a mirror opposite the bed or next to your left.

# 33. Remedy to Knife Bedroom

**A** knife-shaped room is formed when there is an adjacent room or toilet. As most of the *chi* is concentrated at the edge of the knife, it is best not to position yourself here. It does not matter whether the room is being used as an office or bedroom – the effects of bad feng shui remain.

However, if you have no choice and end up at the edge of the knife, there are a few measures you can take to ward off the blows of the chopper.

## Mirror Solution
Placing a mirror opposite to reflect your image towards the handle will help to neutralise the effects of bad feng shui.

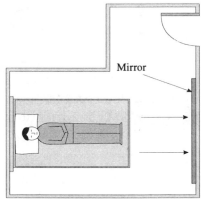

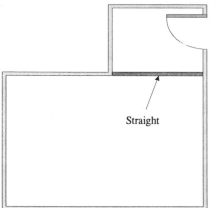

## Line Solution
Draw a straight line on the floor to cut off the handle and help balance up the room.

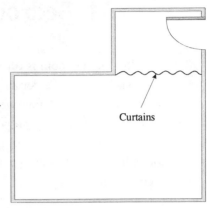

## Curtain solution
You can put up a curtain as an alternative.

Curtains

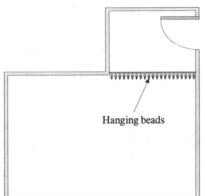

Hanging beads

## Hanging Beads Solution
Hanging beads can ward off the effects of bad feng shui.

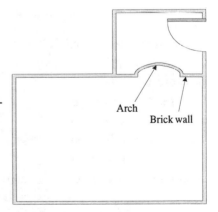

## Arch Solution
A brick arch offers a permanent solution.

Arch

Brick wall

# 34. Bedroom Ceiling

The ceiling in our room is often called the internal sky. This flat or uneven layer with its external roofing protects us from the changing *chi* around us. However, each time we take to the bed, our artificial sky has a bearing on us. If the ceiling is not properly balanced, the *chi* coming from that direction would be unbalanced, thus giving us a restless night. Let us take a closer look at how the different types of ceilings can affect our well-being when we retire for the night.

## The Full Slant

This ceiling has double the adverse effects of the half slant ceiling as the slope is much steeper. Thus *chi* flows more forcefully from one end of the ceiling to the other, resulting in more negative effects on the victim.

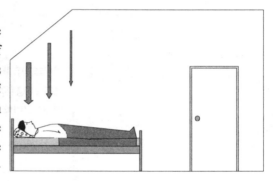

## The Half Slant

This is an unbalanced ceiling because the pressure of *chi* is greater at the end of the slope. If a person were to place his head at this point, he is unlikely to have a good night's rest and

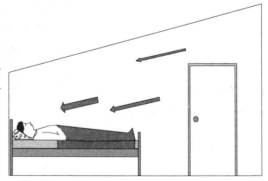

might suffer from headaches and migraines.

## Pyramid Ceiling

A pyramid or any other shape that is found pointing towards a room is bad feng shui. As all sharp points carry lots of *sha chi*, such a shape would produce an over-charged negative force bringing disharmony to the room.

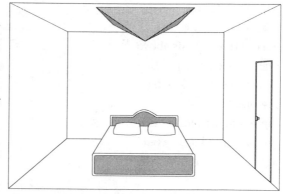

## High and Low Ceiling

When the room has an uneven ceiling, the flow of *chi* will also be unevenly distributed. The part of the room with a lower ceiling will have a heavier concentration of *chi*. Thus whatever portion of the body placed there would be affected by the imbalance.

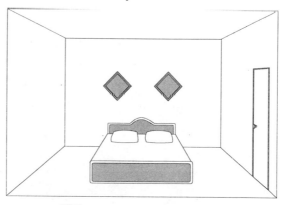

## Safe Ceiling

A safe ceiling is one which is even throughout. As *chi* can flow more evenly in this room, good feng shui is enjoyed by the occupant.

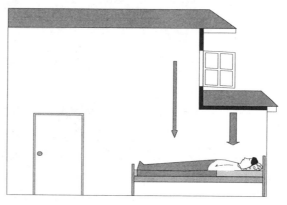

**The Arch Ceiling**

An arch ceiling which curved downwards above one's sleeping position creates unevenness affecting one's feng shui. Placing a small round mirror on the curved area would help to overcome the problem.

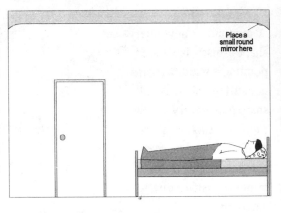

Place a small round mirror here

# 35. Lighting in Bedroom

**M**any of us may not give much thought to where we place the lights in our bedroom. Where the electrical wires protrude forming a break in the wall, there we would fix our lighting as it seems the most convenient point.

To the uninitiated, any place seems like a good place to fix the light as long as it suits his taste. But a geomancer sees things in a different light. If a light is badly placed or out of balance with the bed, it might spell trouble for the occupants.

For a married couple, it could lead to a breakdown in their relationship, whilst for a single person, it could bring problems at work and in one's personal life.

**Middle Placing** (single bed)

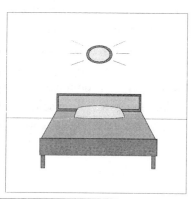

A strong light should not be placed directly above the bed where the head of a person rests because the bright light might be bad for his eyes. In the study of acupuncture, there is a strong link between the liver, the gall bladder and the eyes, so both these organs may be affected too.

**Middle Placing** (double single bed)

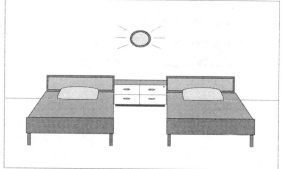

A wall light placed in the centre between two single beds has a well-balanced feng shui.

## On the Left Side

A wall light placed on the left side of the bed, which is the Dragon's side, has strong, good feng shui. Thus the occupants will be blessed with good luck.

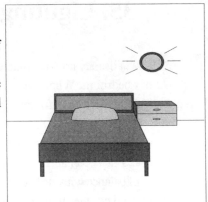

## On the Right Side

A wall light should never be placed on the right side of the bed as this is the domain of the White Tiger. A wall light placed on this side would put the White Tiger in a dominant position over the Dragon. The result: lots of quarrels and misunderstandings between couples.

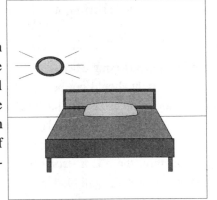

## Too Much on the Left

When using two wall lights, one of them should not be placed too much on the left of the bed as this would result in an imbalance.

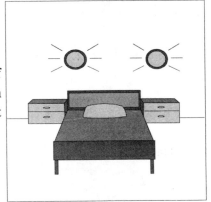

**Too Much on the Right**

Similarly, do not fix one of the lights too much to the right side of the bed. It is certainly not good for harmonious living.

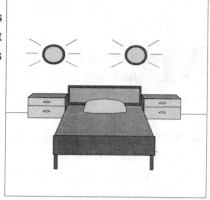

**Well Balanced**

This is an illustration of the well-balanced lighting which generates a very positive atmosphere and promotes harmony in the house.

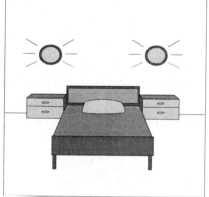

# 36. Bed Headboard

**M**an's first bed was probably the cold hard earth upon which he walked daily. The "ceiling" that he stared up at nightly was the dark void above, dotted with millions of stars in dust-like formation. It was later that straws and hay came into the picture to make sleep more comfortable for the tired mind and body.

As time went by, the bed was elevated – a flat rectangular wooden platform with four wooden pegs was among the first beds that took shape. Crude it may be, but it helped to keep scorpions, snakes and other creepy crawlies at bay.

The bed has come a long way since the days of yore. Today, as the modern bed presents itself in different forms to pander to man's increasing demands for comfort and luxury, the lore of feng shui dictates that the shape of a headboard can reinforce positive energy or drain vital *chi* from its user.

We take a look at a few common shapes for headboards and see how they fare where feng shui is concerned.

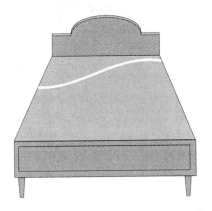

**Curved-in-the-middle headboard brings good feng shui.**

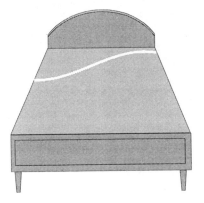

**Curved-from-end-to-end headboard bears good feng shui.**

A double-curve headboard shows individuality. But since its curves are harmonious, relationships are not badly affected for its users.

Tombstone headboard – A high arched headboard on a single bed looks like a tombstone, thus giving off negative vibes to its user.

A fire headboard gives off a mild energy of courage and strength. Recommended for the weak and timid who are looking for some inner strength.

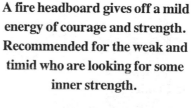

**Triangle**
Such a shape should be avoided because the triangle emanates "invisible heat" – bad feng shui that brings quarrel and disagreement to the user.

## Gremlin

Brings nightmares to whoever sleeps in a bed with this headboard.

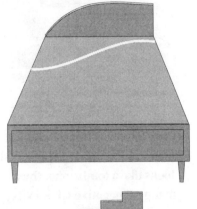

### Quarter-shape

Bad feng shui as the sides are not balanced.

### Step Ladder (1)

Steps on a headboard can mean going up or down. It is best to avoid such a headboard as one's life can go either way.

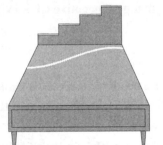

### Step Ladder (2)

Some parents would like to have such a headboard for their children who share the same bedroom. Since it is similar to the step ladder (1) headboard with steps that go either way, it is best not to use such a headboard.

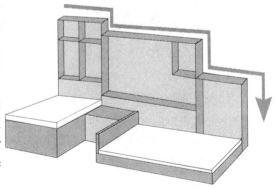

**Dragon and Phoenix**

A headboard which has one side higher is known as the "dragon and phoenix" headboard. For harmony, the male should sleep on the side where the headboard is higher.

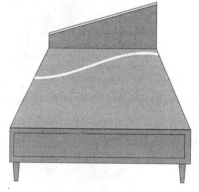

**Slant**

Unlike the gentle curve of a dragon and phoenix headboard, one that slants is bad feng shui as it denotes luck going downwards.

**Fan**

Fan headboard is in a shape of a fan as well as that of a moon. This shape symbolises that nature is at play, so those using a bed with this headboard will have restful sleep.

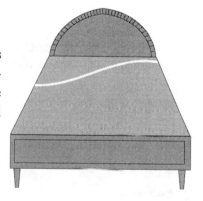

**Seashell**

Like the fan, the sea shell also brings good feng shui because of its harmonious shape.

115

## Low

If the headboard is less prominent and lower than where the feet are, it is bad feng shui because the feet should not supersede the head.

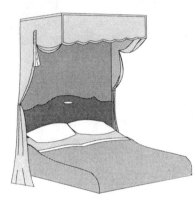

## Prominence

This bed has a good headboard backed by a prominent top. Good feng shui that brings honour and recognition.

## Out of Proportion

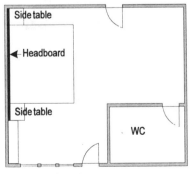

Headboard longer than the length of the bed

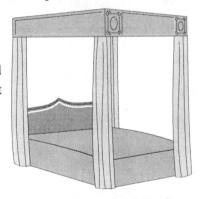

## Enclosed

Such antique-type bed with a good headboard has good feng shui because the user is protected.

Similarly to a human head that is supported by a full-length body, the headboard should not be longer than the bed itself. To sleep in a bed with a bigger headboard would thus cause instability in a relationship. The remedy is to make the headboard shorter, in proportion to the bed.

# 37. Position of Your Study Table

Whether one is a student or not is immaterial but the study table in the bedroom where one does his writing or literary work must be positioned properly. Otherwise, a "bad spot" for the table would affect one's concentration on work. Where one places the study table is important because a proper position would enhance mental strength and concentration.

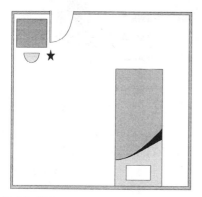

**Behind Door**
The opening door would knock against the table.

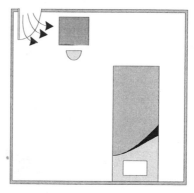

**Beside Door**
Whenever the door is opened, the burst of *chi* into the room would affect concentration.

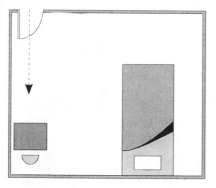

**Facing Door**
One ends up facing violent *chi* directly.

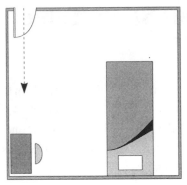

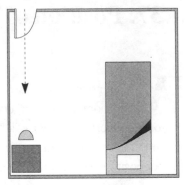

### Side to Door

*Chi* entering the room would still affect the person working at the table.

### Back to Door

The person ends up with his blind side exposed.

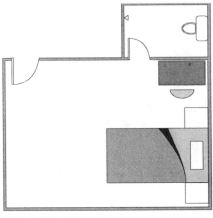

### Next to WC

Placing the study table next to the toilet is bad feng shui because *sha chi* can penetrate the wall towards the study area.

### Facing Window

A position away from the door is good feng shui as it is away from disturbance. If there is a garden to provide a soothing view, having a desk that faces the window is a bonus.

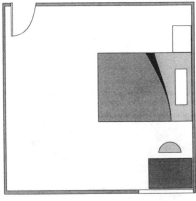

118

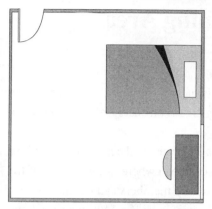

### Next to Bed
A study table next to the bed and facing the window with a good view is good feng shui.

## Cut by clothesline
If the study table is in a good position, do not string a clothesline above it, otherwise the line would create a guillotine effect and cause disharmony for the user.

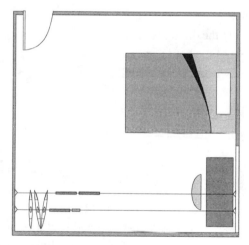

# 38. The Dining Area

The dining area is where the family gathers to enjoy a good meal. In the practice of feng shui, the dining area is an energy point representing the hub of the family.

Just like the stomach which is centrally located in the human anatomy, so too the dining area should be well placed somewhere in the middle of the house. It should be placed where the family members can partake of their food in peace and comfort, so that they can be sufficiently nourished and strengthened to take on the daily challenges of life.

We take a look at some of the positions to avoid when deciding where to place the dining table.

### Facing the Front Door
It is believed that placing the dining table towards the front portion of the house and exposing it to outside view, one's wealth will be lost.

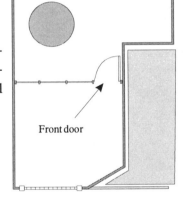

Front door

### Facing the Toilet
The well-being and health of the occupants may be affected if the dining table faces the toilet. If it is not possible to change the position of the toilet door, then put up a wooden partition to block the view of the WC.

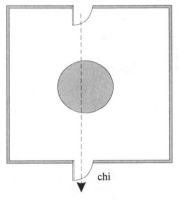

### In Line with Doors

If the dining table is in line with two facing doors, any wealth that comes into the house will be quickly dispersed. In such a situation, place a wind chime along the doorway to slow down the flow of *chi*.

chi

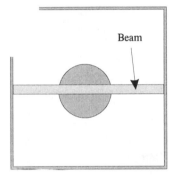

Beam

### Under a Beam

The occupants of the house would find it hard to earn a living if the dining table is under a beam. It is as if their livelihood is being "weighed down".

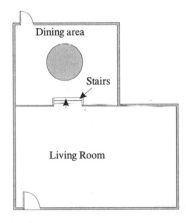

Dining area

Stairs

Living Room

### On Lower Ground

A dining area that is lower than the living room denotes a downhill ride in your quest to seek a comfortable living. If the ceiling is high enough, level up the dining area with the living room. If that is not practical, then place a mirror on the ceiling of the dining area, to raise the *chi* in that part of the house.

121

## Small Corner

It is believed that placing the dining table in a small corner, one's food is being squeezed out. To enhance the dining area, place mirrors along the wall in line with the dining table to create an illusion of space for better harmony.

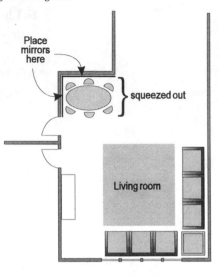

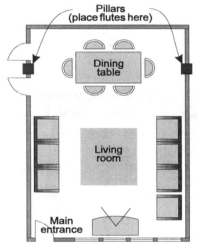

## Between Two Pillars

As a dining area is where food is served, it is bad feng shui to be located between two pillars as one's earnings would be sandwiched. To rectify this situation, place two flutes on each pillar to siphon off *sha chi*.

## In Line with Doors

As *chi* tends to travel in a straight line, to have two doors in a straight alignment and your dining table between them would cause much wealth to escape. One can move the dining table away from the main door and at the same time place a partition as shown in the illustration.

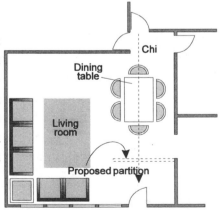

**Risk of Contamination**

*Chi* that enters the front door and comes through the house would find its way out via the toilet. When *chi* passes through the toilet window and across the dining table, it would contaminate the food on the table. Thus the best way is to use the dining table that is found in the dining area instead of in the kitchen area.

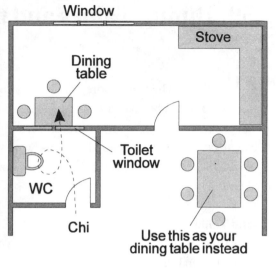

Window

Stove

Dining table

Toilet window

WC

Chi

Use this as your dining table instead

# 39. Dining Tables and their Shapes

T he times when the entire family gets together are usually during breakfast, lunch and dinner, and that means around the dining table. In feng shui, the design of the dining table has an impact on the relationship between family members; good designs would promote harmony in the household while badly designed tables would cause much bickering within the family.

### Round Table
Because the circular shape has no beginning or end, this design is perfect and such a table is referred to as the "heavenly table". Good feng shui.

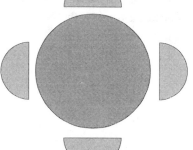

### Oval Table
Other than the round table, the oval table is also deemed good feng shui.

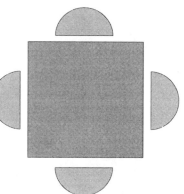

### Square Table
This design is neither good nor bad.

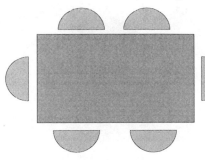

### Rectangular Table

As with the square table, this design is neutral.

### Long Table

Mainly for banquets, one needs to have a large house in order to have such a dining table, which certainly would not fit common houses nowadays. Feng shui wise, it would not be conducive to have this type of table unless you have an extremely large family. As the saying goes: *wear the hat that fits*.

### Fan Shape

A fan-shaped table is not a well-balanced table, thus it will not benefit one to own such a table.

## Quarter Shape

The quarter-shaped table shares the same significance as the fan-shaped table. Because it is half the size of the fan-shape, it has double the adverse effects.

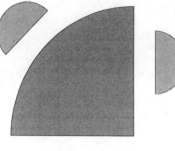

## Triangle Shape

As the triangle is the symbol of the fire element, you are likely to court trouble with such a table.

## Eight-sided Table

This table is rare as it has to be specially ordered due to its odd shape. Like a *pat kua*, a symbol of protection to ward off evil, each of the eight sides carries a different significance. Those who sit at the different angles are imbued with different elements. Thus family members end up with conflicting opinions. Besides, the sharp angles also emit *sha chi*. All said, it is best to avoid an eight-sided table.

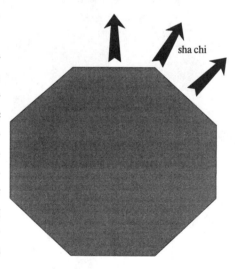

sha chi

## L-Shaped Table

The L-shaped table is usually found attached to a built-in cabinet in the kitchen. The weak point here lies at the end of the "L" as whoever sits there would be placed in a vulnerable position.

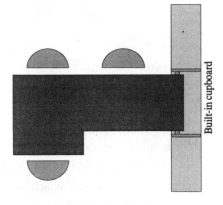

## Glass Table

As glass is transparent, light can pass through and so can *chi*. As a dining table is a place where food is served, a glass top will enable food to "fall through". So avoid a table with a glass top and opt for a round wooden table instead.

# 40. The Kitchen

**T**he kitchen is often known as the hub of family life for it is here that food is prepared so that all members may be nourished by it. Those who love to cook spend more time in the kitchen than in any other part of the house, except for the bedroom, of course.

In ancient China, it was taboo to have a bedroom too near the kitchen. The reason being that firewood, which was used for cooking then, would release carbon and other noxious fumes that pose a health hazard to those sleeping next door. Besides, any outbreaks of fire were likely to start in the kitchen.

Let us look at some of the places to avoid when locating a kitchen, so that harmony and good fortune may be bestowed on the family.

## In the Front

Never have a kitchen at the front of your house as it may give others the impression that food is always first on your mind. Besides, in feng shui practice, a kitchen at the front would mean that wealth (as symbolised by food) would be lost easily.

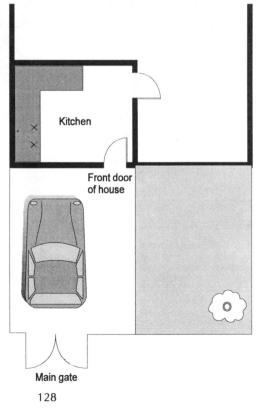

Kitchen

Front door
of house

Main gate

128

## Open Kitchen

Just as warm food needs to be covered after it is cooked, a kitchen with an open top spells bad feng shui as it is exposed to the natural elements.

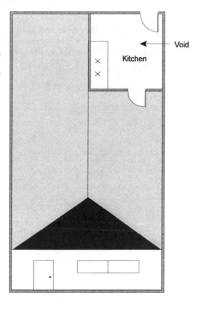

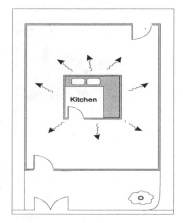

## In the Middle

A kitchen smack in the middle of the house is bad feng shui as heat or energy from the kitchen would be distributed throughout the house. That being the case, you can expect lots of strife and quarrels among family members.

## Back Location

A kitchen located at the back of the house generally has good feng shui as the "cooking heat" or energy is placed away from the main frame of the house. Besides that, waste from the kitchen can be easily disposed off from the back of the house.

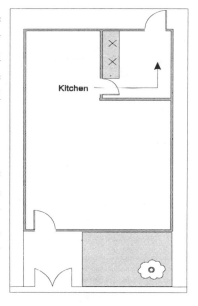

129

## Glass Rooftop

Negativeness hovers over a kitchen with a glass rooftop. As glass is transparent, whatever good feng shui there may be in the kitchen will be lost due to the exposure to the sky.

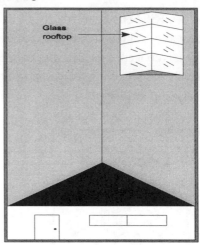

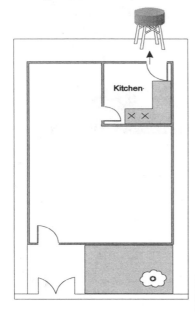

## By the Side

A kitchen located by the side of the house near the back is fine. Such a placing is most suitable for semi-detached houses or bungalows as heat, fumes and gases from the kitchen can be easily dispersed from the house.

## Facing Water Tower

Even though this kitchen is well-positioned at the back of the house, its back faces a water tower. This is considered bad feng shui because the water element will clash with the fire element from the stove, thus destroying the harmony of the kitchen.

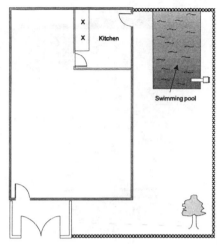

Kitchen

X
X

Swimming pool

## Facing Swimming Pool

Even though this kitchen is nicely located at the back of the house, its harmony is destroyed by the direct confrontation with the swimming pool. The water element will clash with the fire element from the stove.

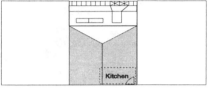

Main road

Kitchen

Back lane

## Back to Back

A kitchen should have a good backing that reflects firm support. If the back of the kitchen faces the back of another, then it can be said that the kitchen has a neutral backing as it is backed by its own kind.

## No Backing

If the back of the kitchen faces a back lane, this is bad feng shui as the kitchen does not have a proper backing. The situation will be aggravated if dirty water from the drain flows towards the house. Bad luck may come your way.

Kitchen

Main road

No backing

Back lane    Flow of dirty water    Kitchen

Main road

131

## Facing Back Lane with a Backing

Not all kitchens facing the back lane will have bad feng shui. There are exceptions, of course. If the drain water flows away from the house, and there is a hill or higher ground at the end of the junction, then these very factors provide a favourable atmosphere for the kitchen.

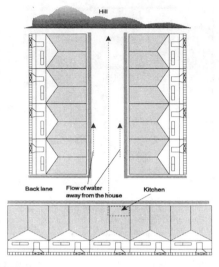

## On First Floor

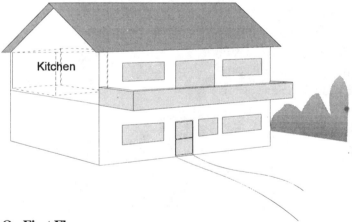

A kitchen should never be situated on the first floor of the bungalow unless there is another kitchen directly below to support it. This is because the fire element (from the stove) is a volatile element and needs to rest on the earth element as represented by the ground.

# 41. Positioning the Stove
# (Dos and Don'ts)

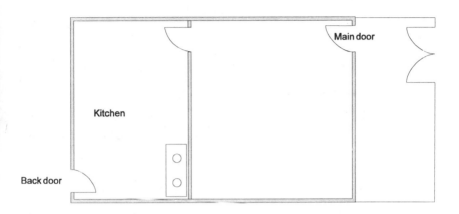

## Facing the Door

A stove that faces the main door of the house symbolises food going out from the front. Similarly, if the cooker faces the back door, it would symbolise food going out from that direction.

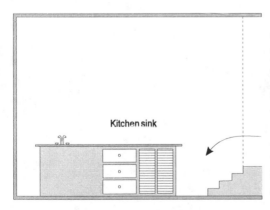

## Going Down

If the kitchen is at a level lower than the living and dining areas, the occupants would find it hard to prosper since the daily "descent" into the kitchen would signify one's slide down the economic ladder.

## Below the Toilet

The toilet should never be situated above the stove on the ground floor; it would be like having waste flushed down into your rice bowl, bringing with it bad feng shui.

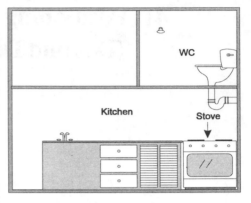

## Water Tank Above

The stove symbolises the fire element, whilst the water tank carries with it the water element. By having the water tank above the stove, the water element is allowed to dominate the fire element, thus extinguishing the flame on your stove. Hence you are unlikely to find prosperity in life.

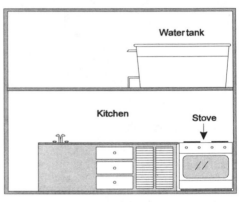

## Bedroom Above

As heat rises from the stove, a bedroom situated on a floor above the stove will feel the heat from below. Such a bedroom is unsuitable for those who are bad tempered or easily agitated. If this is something that cannot be helped, you can paint the walls green to cool down this "fire" room.

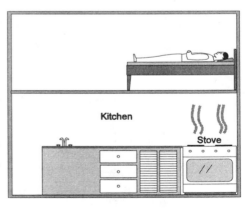

134

## Beam Over Cooker

Never place your cooker beneath a concrete beam as it exerts a negative force on your stove. As the stove represents your rice bowl, you might find it hard to eke out a decent living.

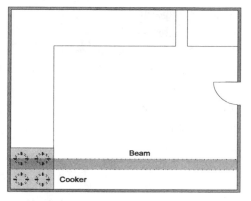

## Next to Window

If your cooker is backed by a window, it is in a vulnerable position. Wind from outside can easily extinguish the flame on your stove, so there is no guarantee of a good livelihood.

## Facing Store Room

A cooker should not be placed facing the store room where brooms, old shoes and old newspapers are kept.

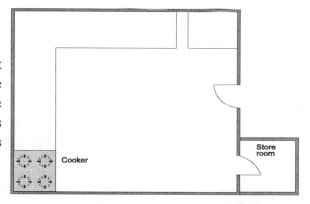

135

## Facing Refrigerator

A refrigerator symbolises a state of stagnation as frozen food is kept inside. As such, it is not good for the stove to face it, as your food supply for the family could "freeze up" too.

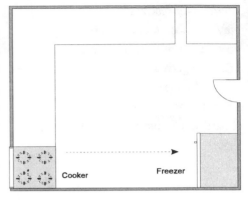

## Facing Toilet

The constant flushing of the toilet after use will signify food being flushed away if you place your cooker opposite the toilet.

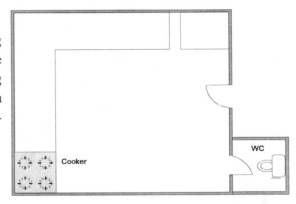

## Water versus Fire

A cooker should not face the wash basin since one represents the fire element while the other signifies for the water element. As water can extinguish fire, your livelihood might be adversely affected if your cooker faces the wash basin.

136

## Beggar Position

A beggar seeking alms would often jiggle his begging bowl, causing the coins inside to jingle. The cooker can be said to assume the "beggar position" if it is situated next to the door. Each time the door opens and bangs against it, the cooker gets a rude knock.

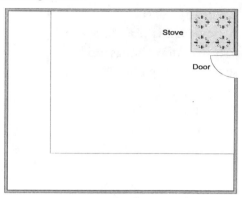

## Facing Staircase

A stove that faces the staircase is bad feng shui as you have to confront it whenever you use the staircase. As the stove represents the fire element, you can expect to run head-on into lots of problems.

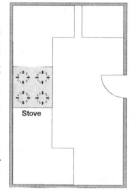

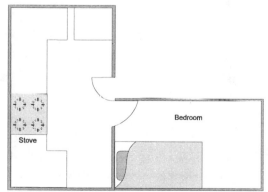

## Facing Bedroom

Having a bedroom next to the kitchen is bad enough, but if the stove faces its door, that is even worst. You can avert the problem by moving the stove away to another spot and turning the bedroom into a storeroom.

## Backed by Toilet

A stove that is placed back-to-back to the toilet brings bad feng shui even though the toilet cannot be seen from the kitchen. The constant flushing of the toilet after use symbolises food going down the drain.

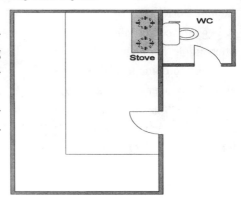

## Sewage Foundation

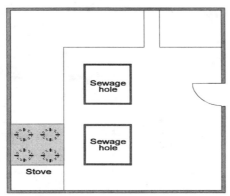

Due to renovations to the house, the extended kitchen may now sit on what was once the sewage hole. As waste is discharged into the hole, a kitchen with such a foundation has bad feng shui.

## Below Water Pipe

The water pipe that leads to the sink should not be higher than the stove. Otherwise, the water would extinguish the fire on the stove, thus depriving the family of its food supply or source of livelihood.

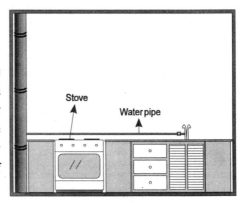

138

## Undermined by Drainage

A drainage system that flows below the cooking area bears the
same symbolism of water extinguishing the fire on the stove.
Avoid this situation.

## The North

Never place your stove facing
North as this is the direction of
the water element. As the fire on
your stove could succumb to the
water element, this could make life
difficult for your family.

## The South

The South belongs to the fire element. There is a difference of opin-
ion here among feng shui experts.
Some believe that the stove should
not face the fire element as too much
heat would be generated within the
household. Others hold that the
South is a neutral direction and it is
safe to place the cooker here.

I believe the South is a good alternative, for want of a better choice. A
word of caution though: if you are
running a restaurant, then avoid this
direction as constant use of the stove
can easily cause too much heat all
around.

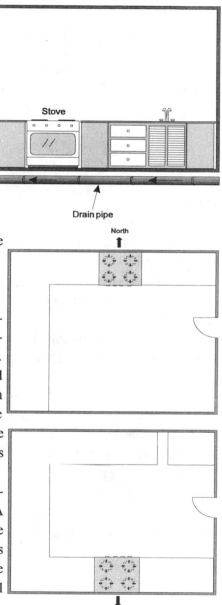

Stove

Drain pipe

North

South

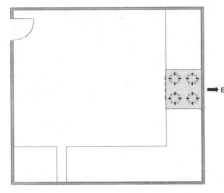

## The East

East is the best direction to face as this belongs to the wood element. As wood is fuel for fire, you can be → East assured that everything will run smoothly where business and career are concerned.

## The West

The West is in the metal area. Here again experts have differing opinions. Some argue that our cooker and oven are made mostly West ← of metal, so it is fine to face the West.

I have my doubts though; I think it is best not to face this direction.

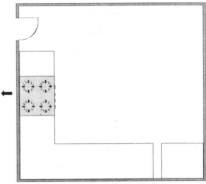

## The Centre

The centre of the kitchen belongs to the Earth element. As Earth itself can snuff out a flame, do not place your cooker in the centre, otherwise you might have to struggle to make ends meet.

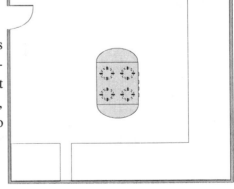

**Must Have a Back Door**

All houses that have a front door must have a back door to allow stale *chi* to flow out. A house without a back door would be choking with negative *chi* that may affect the progress and health of the occupants. There are lots of wastes that need to be disposed of from the kitchen, so it is always better to have the back door in the kitchen. However, if the back door cannot be located in the kitchen for some reason, it is still better to have a back door elsewhere than to do without one.

# 42. Toilet

In the old days, there were no such things as toilets. People either dug a hole in the ground, or did it in the bush or behind a tree.

During the 17th century in Europe, because of poor hygiene and sanitation, bubonic plague broke out, known as the Black Death. The disease caused people to bleed in the skin and was so devastating that one-fourth of the European population was wiped out. In London alone, 50,000 people perished.

Locally, during the pre-war years, the bucket system was implemented in urban areas. Having a bucket latrine seemed a luxury at that time. Sewerage facilities improved when pipes were laid in the ground to carry sewage away from homes, to be deposited in a collection centre elsewhere.

Today, there are toilets in almost every home, making the task of disposing bodily wastes so convenient and hygienic. But in many parts of China and Third World countries, there is still no proper toilet. If one were to visit certain parts of China, one should bring along two umbrellas in case nature calls; if there is no toilet around, you can set up your own by opening the two umbrellas and using them to shield you from others' eyes!

Toilets at home, like the human anatomy, are always situated at the rear. As everything on earth must have its rightful place, a well-placed toilet would ensure harmony in the house. On the other hand, a badly placed toilet would have adverse effects on the household.

The other day, I had the opportunity to observe the effects of a toilet next to a room. Having bought a framed photograph of the late Bruce Lee, a collector's item from the United States, I left it in a cupboard which was against the wall separating the room from the toilet. A week later, I found moss growing on the cupboard — moisture from the toilet had penetrated the wall.

Therefore, if a man were to position his bed in the spot where the cupboard is and sleep there, after some time, his body would absorb too much *yin chi* from the toilet and end up with arthritis.

Toilets at home, like the human anatomy, are always situated at the rear of the house. As everything on earth must have its rightful place, a well-placed toilet would ensure harmony in the house. On the other hand, a badly placed toilet would have adverse effects on the household.

**Facing main door**
Having a toilet that faces the main door is to face misfortune always.

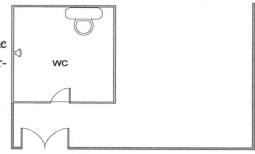

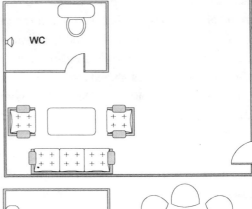

**Facing Living Room**

Friendship would never last.

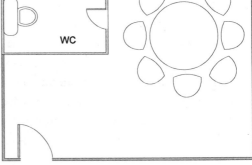

**Facing Dining Area**

One would find it hard to make a living.

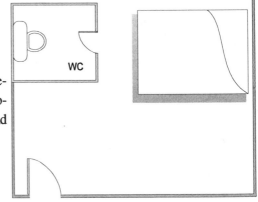

**Facing Bed**

Exposure to bad *chi* and bacteria as these would flow towards the bed, one's nose and lungs would be infected.

### Sleeping below toilet

When there is a toilet above your bed, you can expect bad luck.

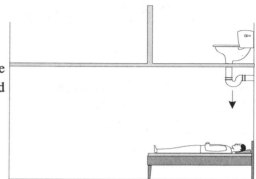

### Next to Toilet

One who sleeps next to the wall separating the toilet would absorb *yin chi* and dampness.

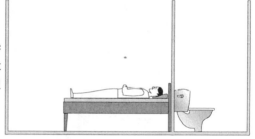

### Aquarium next to Toilet

Having an aquarium of fish in the house brings in luck. But to place it next to the toilet can cause losses because the toilet is where water (*sui*) is flushed away, therefore wealth would be drained away.

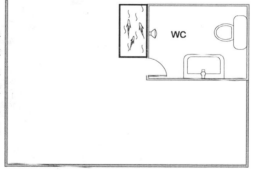

# 43. The Placement of Aquarium

**R**earing fish in an aquarium at home is a popular hobby. Having such an aquarium in the house not only beautifies the home environment, it also acts as a "tonic" for the tired mind, for gazing at fish swimming leisurely in their tank can be quite a soothing experience. But to businessmen and others, placing an aquarium in the house is to improve wealth, fortune and happiness.

We shall identify areas at home where the aquarium can be placed to enhance one's well-being.

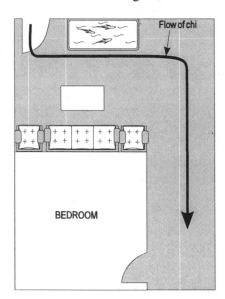

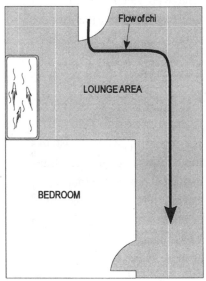

**Where the Door Opens**
This is a good position as the aquarium "welcomes" wealth to the house.

**Behind the Door**
*Chi* flows past the aquarium and into the house.

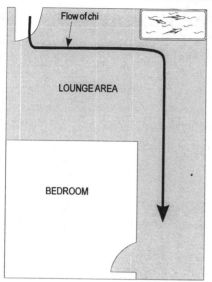

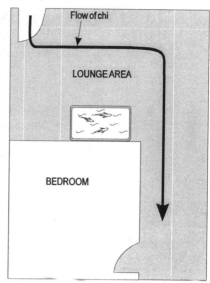

## In a Corner

This placing symbolises one "secretly receiving luck".

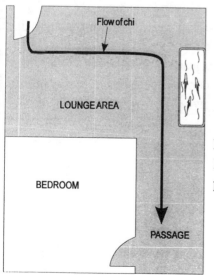

## At the Lounge Area

An aquarium placed in the lounge area and not directly facing the main door is good, as *chi* is "dragged" into the house.

## Near Passageway

Enhances fortune for all at home, especially the head of the house.

# 44. The Negative Placement of Aquarium

**T**here are also areas where the aquarium should not be placed, otherwise the effect would be adverse.

### Facing Main Door

To have the aquarium directly facing the main entrance is bad feng shui, as one's wealth would flow out.

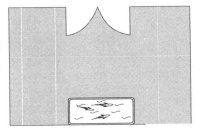

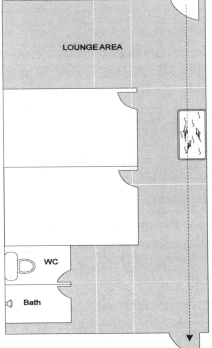

### Between Openings

*Chi* travels swiftly in a straight line from door to door. By placing the aquarium in between, wealth that comes into the house is easily flushed away.

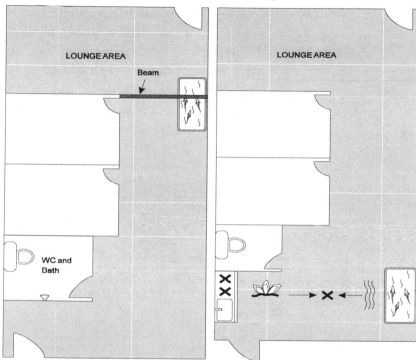

## Under a Beam

A beam exerts greater atmospheric pressure than other parts of the roof, therefore to have a beam above the aquarium is akin to weighing down one's luck and wealth.

## Facing Kitchen

The cooking area has fire and water. As these elements would strive to dominate one another, such conflict would bring financial problems to the house owner.

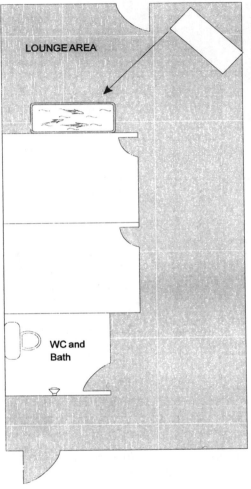

LOUNGE AREA

WC and
Bath

**Facing Sharp Angles**
Improperly placed furniture would cause *sha chi* to angle towards the aquarium resulting in financial woes. In this case, it is best to rearrange the furniture.

# 45. Wind Chimes

**W**ind chimes may make music in the wind, but beware of the type of wind chime you have hanging in your house. While some may bring good luck to the owner, there are certain designs which you should avoid at all cost.

### Bell Chime
This kind of wind chime is best for temples and monasteries; it is not suitable for residential houses as it has the tendency to attract spirits to reside within.

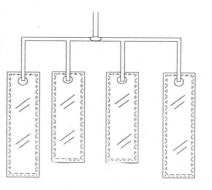

### Oblong Chime
The oblong chime takes the shape of metal strips. As its sides look like the edges of a razor, it is best to avoid such a design as it would cut up one's luck.

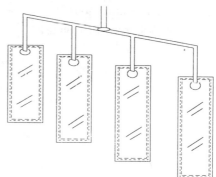

### Uneven Chime
An uneven chime will swing wildly in the wind. Thus *chi* will be unevenly distributed in the house. Certainly not the type of wind chime you should hang in your house.

### Pagoda Wind Chime

As pagoda shapes are believed to have the power to disperse evil forces and *sha chi*, such a wind chime would benefit the home owner.

### Round-tube Chime

As round shapes represent the heavenly shape, having a wind chime with round tubes will chase away bad luck and bring good tidings to the owner.

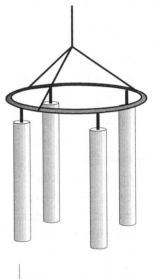

### Fish Chime

The fish motif has been widely used as decorative images in China since ancient times. They can be found in pottery, carved bones, stones, brocade and even jade. The vivid figure and elegant shape of the fish make it a popular item in traditional Chinese decoration.

The Chinese like the fish, all the more so since "fish" and "abundance" share similar sounds — *yee* — in Cantonese. So having a wind chime decorated with a fish at the top and bottom, symbolises good tidings.

# 46. How to Position a Wind Chime

**B** ells placed strategically in temples and monasteries have always been a common sight in China. The primary purpose of ringing the bells was to call for prayer and to signify other temple activities. Bells were also rung to call for help in case of fires or an uprising in the empire.

*Fung ling* (wind chimes) – or miniature "bells" as they are known in feng shui – consists of thin strips of metal or ceramic which, when moved by the wind, would create melodious sound as they knock against one another.

In feng shui, the sound of *fung ling* bells creates a pathway linking the spirit world to the physical realm. Taoists and Buddhists believe that the sound of the bells in the daytime helps to produce a powerful vibration which disperses negative elements, thereby protecting the temple premises. Apparently, temple *fung ling* bells also provide a lodging place for sad and wandering spirits during the night.

The main purpose of *fung ling* is to slow down the forceful flow of *chi* that passes through doorways and windows. The movement of the *fung ling* also helps to disperse *chi* to other parts of the house, thus benefiting those neglected areas.

In purchasing a *fung ling*, one should first test it for its sound, by shaking it. If the sound is pleasant and soothing, the *fung ling* is good. On the other hand, if the *fung ling* gives off a dull or sharp sound that jangles the nerves, then that *fung ling* is unsuitable for one's house as it would make one increasingly uncomfortable as time goes by.

In deciding where to place the *fung ling*, one has to study the situation of the house carefully. Otherwise, hanging it in the wrong place would bring ill luck instead of harmony.

### Placed at the Opening

Placing a *fung ling* near the opening of the door is not good because upon opening the door, forceful *chi* would cause the *fung ling* to swing out of control. The diverted *chi* is thus not well distributed inside.

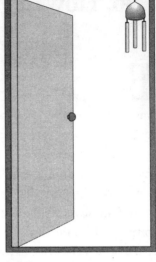

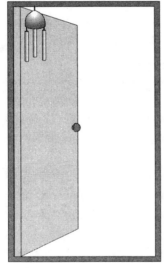

### Placed near the joint

As most doors won't be opened fully when a person enters the premises, placing a *fung ling* near the joint of the door would not help to arrest the flow of *chi*. As such, this positioning is not effective.

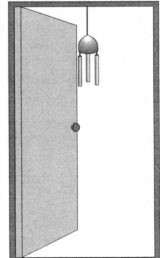

### Kowtowing to the House

A *fung ling* should not hang too low, otherwise one would have to duck to avoid it; this gesture is likened to kowtowing to one's house. This is not advisable.

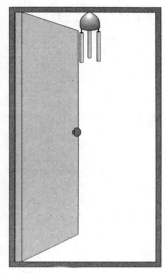

### Fixed *fung ling*

A *fung ling* should not be fixed in such a way that it cannot be moved even by the slightest wind. In such a case, it has no function except as an ornament.

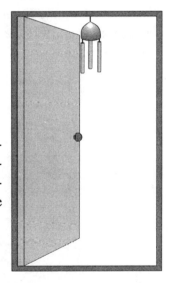

### Central Position

A *fung ling* should be placed in a central position along the ledge of the door so that it can arrest the swift flow of *chi* coming in and distribute it evenly throughout the interior of the house.

# 47. Where to Position a Wind Chime

## Door-to-door Situation

**C**hi would be lost in a situation in which a door faces another door. Thus a *fung ling* placed at the front door would slow down the forces of *chi* coming in and distribute *chi* to other parts of the house.

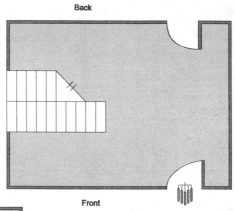

Back

Front

Back

## Three-door Syndrome

Three doors aligned in a straight line also means *chi* is channelled out in a straight line and is thus lost. Here, two wind chimes are required instead of just one.

Front

**Main Door Facing Balcony Door**
This layout is normally found in condominiums and apartments where the main door directly faces the balcony door. A *fung ling* placed at the front door would help to slow down and arrest *chi* to circulate to other parts of the apartment, thus benefiting those areas.

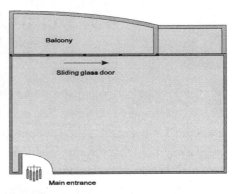

**Door Facing Staircase**
A main door facing the staircase would have *chi* running up the staircase without benefiting the ground floor of the house. As such a *fung ling* should be placed at the front of the main door.

**Main Door Facing Store Room Door**
A main door facing a store room door located underneath a staircase would help to trap immediate *chi* coming in. The trapped *chi* in the store room eventually becomes stale. As dead *chi* facing the main door would not enhance one's luck, a *fung ling* placed at the main door would help to direct *chi* to other section of the house.

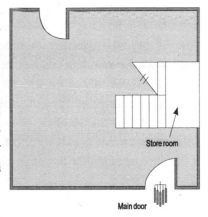

# 48. Beam Burden

Is there a logical explanation why a concrete beam above a person would have a negative effect on him over time? As a practising geomancer, whenever I see a client positioned directly below a beam I suggest that he move away from that position. But if he insists on staying put, then I would wish him the strength of Atlas to bear whatever "burden" that may come his way. Is it a mere superstition that being in the shadow of a beam brings misfortune?

Sometime back, I met a client for the first time and noticed that she had her seat under a beam. I remarked that she had a problem on the right side of her neck and shoulder. She gave me a Cheshire cat-grin, and I knew that I was right. I called on her a couple of days later and saw that her table and seat had been moved out of alignment with the beam. The stiff neck and shoulder that she had carried for so many years were gone.

Another client who had a beam over the head of her bed admitted to having frequent headaches. She changed the position of the bed and her headaches disappeared. I had wondered if it was my advice that did the trick. Then it dawned on me one day that it was really physics.

We know that external pressure on our bodies is equal all over, enabling us to move with ease. But take a denser element, like water. When a car plunges into water, the person in the vehicle should not panic. He should wind down the window a bit to let the water in slowly.

As the water fills up the car, the victim would find it easier to open the door as water pressure from the inside negates the external force. But if he panics and goes for the door, he would find it difficult to open as pressure from outside would thwart his effort.

In the case of air, the law of physics also applies.

## 48. Beam Burden

Thus we can conclude that if we place ourselves under a beam, the uneven distribution of atmospheric pressure would affect the part of our body (under the beam) in the long run.

# 49. Beams with Bad Bearings

C eiling beams have a great bearing on the occupants of a house.

### Beam at Entrance
A beam that lies across the main entrance of a house is considered bad feng shui because luck is being pressed down, even though the house may face a good direction.

### Beam in Living Room
The living room is a place for the family to rest or spend their leisure together. Thus a beam which splits the living room is likely to cause disharmony and quarrels among the members.

### Separation Beam
A beam which cuts the marital bed into half could cause a separation or divorce between a couple.

### Hard Living Beam
A dining table is a place where food is being served. So when a beam from the ceiling falls across the table, the owner of the premises might find it hard to eke out a

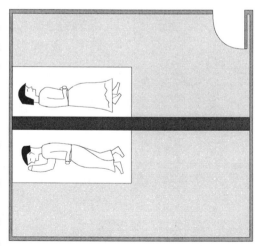

comfortable living for his entire family.

## Beam on Top of Head

A beam that falls on one's head when one is asleep could cause headaches or give the affected party a heavy head.

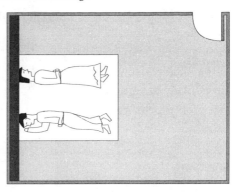

## Bad Finale Beam

As the kitchen door is considered the last door of a house, to have a beam falling in line with the door is like having a bad ending to most matters. If the owner is a businessman, his business deals might suffer a bad ending.

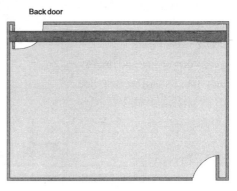

Back door

## Career Problem Beam

A beam which falls over a cooker in the kitchen is considered a stumbling block to one's career.

## Demotion Beam

An executive's room with a beam of uneven level could cause an imbalance of *chi* in the room. Those who have risen high in office might suddenly find a demotion around the corner. Those who are ambitious might find themselves grounded, with bleak prospects of any career advancement.

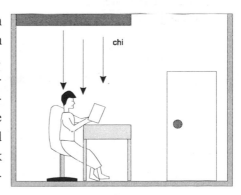

chi

## Blocking Money Beam

As water or *sui* symbolises money, a beam which falls in the middle of a water basin is likely to cause financial problems for the occupants.

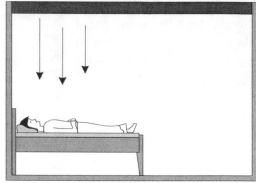

## Solutions

Here are a few suggestions on how to handle bad beams.

## 1. The false panel

If the room has good height, false panels can be installed to create a well-balanced room.

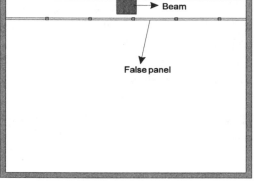

## 2. The firecracker

A red firecracker which symbolises a dynamite can be placed at the centre of the beam to "blast" the beam away.

## 3. Mirror Technique

A small mirror can be placed at the centre of the beam to siphon the unbalanced *chi* from the room.

## 4. Tudor Style

Extra beams could be added to the ceiling beam at equal distances to give the room an aesthetically balanced ceiling *chi*.

# 50. The Airwell
# (The Source of *Yang Chi*)

A void or an airwell created in a house is not simply just a void with no sense of purpose. In fact, if certain parts of a house are too dark and lack ventilation because they are built too far inside, they are considered dead areas. To balance out the darkness, 'void' or airwell are thus built in a house.

As a conduit in channeling natural lights and *yang chi*, life force is brought into the affected areas to nourish the dead rooms and dark areas. We look and see how airwells benefit certain areas in a house when located rightly.

**Airwell in the Front**
Not necessary to have an airwell here as the front bedroom has enough windows for sufficient light and ventilation. However, having an airwell here would not do any harm. If it looks too empty, plant some plants here.

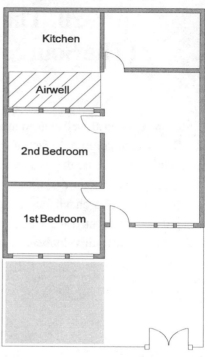

**Between Bedroom and Kitchen**

The location of the airwell benefits mainly the second bedroom and the kitchen area.

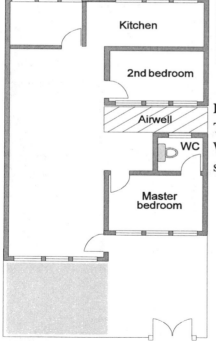

**Between WC and Bedroom**

The location of the airwell benefits the WC of the master bedroom and the second bedroom.

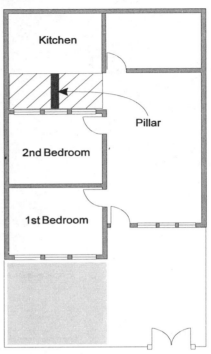

## Yang Chi Split by Pillar

A pillar constructed along the airwell area split the *yang chi* here. As such the energy coming down in the house is uneven.

## In the Kitchen

If a kitchen has sufficient windows for ventilation, an airwell should not be built over it. The reason is that as the kitchen is already a heated area, too much *yang chi* and exposure would cause imbalance in the kitchen area.

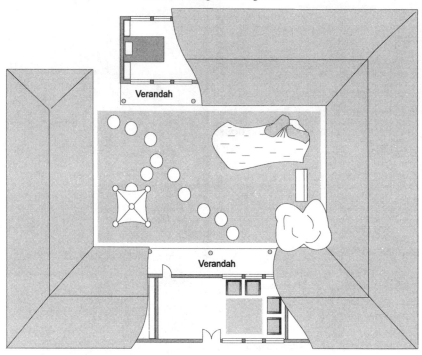

## The Private Void and Internal Garden

Cater for the super-rich, this void is built in the centre of this huge mansion. Within it an internal garden landscape with ponds is constructed solely for the owner to enjoy its serene private atmosphere away from the public eyes. This kind of a void or airwell has very good feng shui as *yang chi* descending from the middle activates this private inner sanctum with life and energy.

# 51. Installing Solar Heater

L ife in modern society offers all kinds of comfort, given the numerous amenities available today. The air-conditioner, water heater, remote control and a host of gadgets all add up to enhance our quality of life. Those of us who use a solar heater to get hot water have to be extra careful not to end up in hot soup.

In feng shui, the solar heater is considered to be of the fire element. By installing a solar heater on our roof-tops to catch the sun's rays, we unwittingly invoke one of the five elements, mainly the water, fire, wood, metal or earth element. That be the case, the heater has to be correctly positioned to enhance the feng shui of the house. If it is ill-placed, bad luck may befall the occupants. We shall take a look at the dos and don'ts when installing a solar heater.

**The Northern Aspect**
The North is the direction of the water element. Since water and fire do not go together, placing a solar heater there would create lots of disharmony and quarrels in the family.

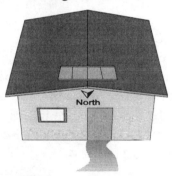

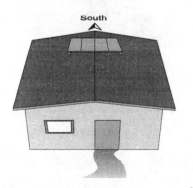

**The Southern Aspect**
The South is of the fire element. Since the solar heater is also of the fire element, this is a neutral area to place the heater as both share the same energy and there are no negative effects.

167

## The Eastern Aspect

The East is represented by the Wood element. Since fire feeds on wood, the East is the best direction to install your solar heater.

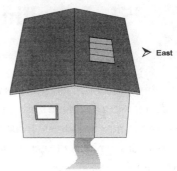

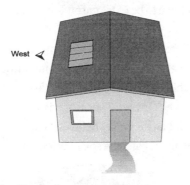

## The Western Aspect

The West is symbolised by the Metal element. Since fire melts metal, fixing the solar heater in this direction will not enhance the feng shui of your house.

## The Centre

The centre of a house represents the earth element. As we know, when earth is placed over a fire, the fire will be snuffed out due to lack of oxygen. So this is not an ideal location for your heater.

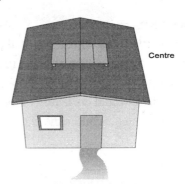

# 52. Installing Ventilators

### In the Centre
Never place a ventilator at the centre of the roof as it will look as though the occupants of the house are unable to take full control of their lives.

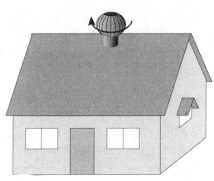

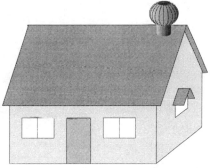

### On the Right
The right side of the house is the dominion of the White Tiger. Placing your ventilator there might make the White Tiger too strong which might create havoc in the family.

### On the Left
If you are using a single ventilator, the best position would be the far left side of the rooftop as it is the Green Dragon area. Placing it there will channel good luck and fortune into your home.

## Equal Level

If your are using two ventilators, do not place them on the same level. If you do, you are giving equal strength or power to the White Tiger and Green Dragon, resulting in a clash or conflict.

## Yin and Yang

higher

If you are going to install two ventilators, place one ventilator higher up the roof on the left side. The other unit can be placed on the right, but at a lower level. Doing this would symbolise that the Green Dragon dominates the White Tiger, thus creating harmony all round.

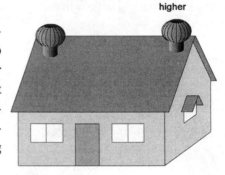

# 53. Green Dragon and White Tiger

**H**ills are considered superior and positive, and are known as *yang* land. Hills which face the right direction are believed to benefit those who live there. History tells us that Rome, situated on seven hills, was founded by the twin brothers Romus and Romula.

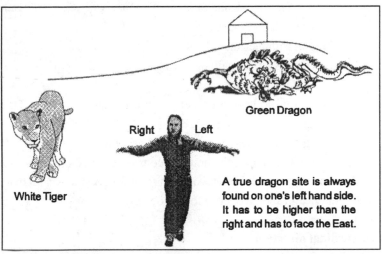

Green Dragon

Right     Left

White Tiger

A true dragon site is always found on one's left hand side. It has to be higher than the right and has to face the East.

There is an interesting story on how Kowloon in Hong Kong came to be named thus. Kowloon means nine dragons in Cantonese, but then it was not built on nine hills. The story goes, once there was a boy emperor who lived in the district. He told his courtier that there were only eight prominent hills, so he could only see eight dragons. He wanted to know how the ninth dragon came about. With respect, the courtier exclaimed, "Ah sir! Surely you must not forget that you yourself is one too." Thus, the name Kowloon came into being.

In feng shui, an ideal spot where the dragon is found is on one's left, where the land must be higher than that on the right. This lower land on the right is called the land of the White Tiger.

However, if the land on the right is higher, this means that the White Tiger will dominate the Green Dragon, thus causing disaster to befall the owner.

A true Dragon site should face the East, or towards the East direction.

If a river or stream runs between the higher and lower ground, the owner can be assured of prosperity.

## 1. The True Dragon

The land on the left hand side of the house which denotes that the Green Dragon is higher than the right side which is the domain of the White Tiger. As such, the

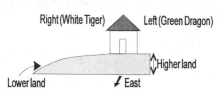

house can be said to have a proper balance because the Green Dragon rightfully dominates the White Tiger.

If this particular house also faces the East or towards the East, which is the Dragon's direction, the house is considered sited on a true dragon area. In this respect this house would warrant for good feng shui in terms of wealth, health and prosperity for the owner.

## Other cardinal direction
## (2) The False Dragon

The land on the left side of a house could be higher than the right side causing the Green Dragon to dominate the White Tiger. However, if the house does not face

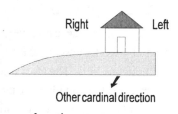

the East, it is considered sited on a false Dragon location.

The owner of this premise still enjoys some kind of benefit but not as great as that of a house sitting on a true Dragon location.

### (3) White Tiger Domination

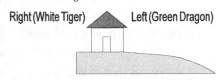

Right (White Tiger)    Left (Green Dragon)

When a land on the right hand side is higher than the left hand side of a house, it denotes that the White Tiger is dominating the Green Dragon. As such, the owner of this particular house would not enjoy any good luck. In fact, his health and wealth would go on a decline due to the imbalances of the White Tiger dominating the Green Dragon.

### (4) Taming the White Tiger

Green Shrubs

The chances of changing the topography of the land to suit one's well-being is not there if one should discover that the right side is higher than the left side. So what can one do if one cannot move out from one's premises where the White Tiger rules supreme over the Green Dragon.

The way out in this situation is to plant green shrubs on the side of the White Tiger. Symbolically, this means feeding the tiger with 'greens'. Thus making the White Tiger a vegetarian instead of a meat eater. This would help to reduce the weight of negativeness towards oneself.

However, one should be cautious not to plant cacti or plants with thorns, otherwise it would be like adding more teeth to the White Tiger to do more harm instead.

### (5) House Found at the Centre

If a house is located on the very top of a piece of land where the left and right slope down equally, it would give the White Tiger and the Green Dragon the same strength.

To create a proper balance, place a boulder on the left hand side of the house to make the Green Dragon more superior.

## (6) White Tiger Attacking Finance

If one has sufficient land on the right side of the house and if the right side is higher than the left , never never place a fountain or a swimming pool in that area. The reason is that as water symbolises wealth, the White Tiger would create havoc towards one's finances.

174

# 54. Planting Your Way to Health

In the old days in China when a man under the age of 80 dies, people would lament that the deceased had had a short life because living till 80 was a norm then. There were also people who had lived past 80 and these centenarians were reckoned as "immortals" who had learnt the secret of longevity.

Today there are some people who have managed to live till such an old age and beyond. This rare breed is normally found in remote highland areas where the air is pure and has lots of negative ions, and the mountain water runs into streams and rivers that are unpolluted. And these people lead carefree and simple lives.

When it comes to harmony for better health, urbanites do not have much because their workplace and residence are mainly in areas where the wheels of development are constantly churning. A man finds it harder to breathe in polluted atmosphere because in such environment the essence of *chi* is less. When the environment changes and where such changes affect you in a negative manner, you can either move away, or make amends to your present situation to counter the changes.

If you find it hard to breathe in your highly-polluted area, you may go green, as in planting. Plants have intrinsic properties that benefit us, and in the feng shui context, plants are often regarded as "natural physicians".

Here is a list of recommended plants:

- **Cape Jasmine**: This plant benefits the liver and gall bladder and helps to cure hepatitis and cholecystitis. The fragrance kills bacteria in the air.
- **Chrysanthemum**: There is an ancient belief that one can achieve longevity by consuming chrysanthemum.

- **Dried Lilac Blossom**: Placing a pouch containing dried lilac blossom in the room helps to prevent pulmonary tuberculosis and chronic gastroenterities. The scent helps to repel mosquitoes.
- **Geranium**: Dissipates fatigue and induces sleep.
- **Herbaceous Peony**: Blooms at 7 am.
- **Honeysuckle**: It is anti-pyretic, and helps to alleviate inflammation.
- **Hyacinth Bean Flower**: Stimulates the appetite.
- **Jasmine**: The fragrance regulates people's *chi*, so that they become more relaxed and cheerful.
- **Lotus**: The bloom spreads its petals at 9 am.
- **Magnolia**: In full bloom by 10 am.
- **Morning Glory**: A timekeeper of nature, as the blooms blossom at 4 am.
- **Sweet-Scented Flowers**: All sweet-scented flowers help to ease a person's mind.

# 55. The Effect of Plants

A house or an apartment can be quite a dull place without the presence of plants. Greenery provides the cosmetic touch, hinting of nature within a man-made environment. There are also plants which bring certain benefits to a home.

**Aloe Vera**
Planting aloe vera around the house can protect the home from intruders. It can also prevent cooking accidents if planted in the kitchen.

**Bromeliads**
This plant has sharp points. It can deflect and diffuse *sha chi* (negative forces), bringing abundance to the home.

**Cactus**
Placed at the windows, the cactus safeguards the house against burglars and intruders. Keeping a pot of cactus in the bedroom helps cool down one's sexual urge.

**Ivy**
Protective as well as decorative, the stem and leaves of the ivy drive off evil forces.

**Orchid**
This plant induces chastity and makes one think of love constantly.

**Palms**
They are also known as "sun plants". They emanate uplifting vibrations.

## Tulip

This flower wards off desperation and poverty. If you save the bulb and re-plant it the following year, love and money would follow.

## Rose

The presence of red roses attracts love to a home. However, a romance may go wrong because of the thorns of the rose. Pain and anguish will result if you let things get out of hand.

# 56. The Power of Trees

One hot afternoon, while walking down a city street with the sun beating down on me, I found myself wishing that tall trees were growing all around. How cool my walk would have been then!

Besides giving us shade and oxygen, trees and their bark are known for their medicinal properties.

While the scientific and practical benefits of having trees around are many, did you know that in the distant past, tree-worship was a common practice? Special groves and sites were reserved as sacred places in ancient Greece, for example, where people could go to give thanks to the tree spirits.

Prince Otto von Bismarck of Germany was known to embrace a favourite tree regularly to replenish his life energy.

Trees act like a two-way radio, receiving and transmitting waves or vibrations. They are believed to emit feelings and emotions, and these in turn are acknowledged by certain "sensitive" people.

Today, communication between man and tree is almost a lost art, known only to a few.

But while some trees can give off friendly emanations, there are others which give off bad vibrations.

In feng shui, it can be determined whether a tree harbours stagnant *chi* and negative forces by the kind of cancerous-looking nodules growing upon their trunks.

Once, while on vacation, I tried to recharge my mental, physical and spiritual "batteries" using a technique that is common among those who believe in the healing power of natural forces. I located a pine tree which had a good source of *chi*, and held up both my hands about 8 centimetres from the trunk. Visualising a link between myself and the tree, I then envisioned a flow of positive energy into my being. After about 10 minutes, I could feel a kind of euphoria and so I made my way back to my apartment feeling much better.

Feedback from trees differs from one to another. Sensitive people will actually tell you that they can feel good and pleasant vibrations from some trees, and ominous signals of gloom and despair from others.

This is a talent that few possess, although if you spend enough time among trees and nature, you may find your own natural senses becoming more attuned to the power of these great plants.

Note, however, that there are some instances in feng shui when a tree on your property may pose a hindrance to your progress or good fortune. In that case, do not hesitate to do what is necessary.

# 57. Animals and Their Significance

**M**any people fear the black cat since the animal is suspected of being a harbinger of ill news, bad luck and misfortune. A brown dog, however, gets a different reception — especially if it appears out of nowhere to take up residence in a household.

Whether or not this is mere superstition, mankind has long believed that animals exert some mysterious karmic force. Below are some of the animals which the art of Chinese divination believes are important:

- **Canary**: Due to its bright yellow colour, the bird is known as sacred to the sun. Kept in the house for its fine song, the canary is believed to promote harmony and happiness. The best in harmony can be achieved by rearing a goldfish beside the canary.
- **Cat**: In Britain, Tibet and Egypt, cats are highly revered. It is known as a mysterious creature because of its nocturnal activities. Its large glowing eyes are believed to be linked to the opaque moon. To ensure good vision and alleviate eye irritation, stroke the tail of a black cat (unless, of course, if you are allergic to cats!). If a cat rests with its tail towards North or East, a storm is on the way. If it washes its face, a visitor will arrive shortly. A tortoise-shell cat shields a home from harm while a smutty-nosed one brings wealth.
- **Cricket**: They are popular pets in the Orient, often kept in metal cages by the hearth. They promote mirth and plenty.
- **Dog**: The dog is revered by ancient peoples such as the Egyptian and the Babylonian. The Chinese believe that the dog is easily spooked by ghosts and spirits. It howls in the acknowledgement of such unseen manifestation. To calm your dog down place your shoe rightside down.

- **Toad**: The toad was once a more popular pet than the dog or the cat. It is supposed to be a bearer of intelligence and protection. It is also highly sensitive to the supernatural world.

- **Turtle**: There is a saying that if one wanted some luck, pat a turtle shell. The turtle is a symbol of longevity and fertility.

- **Fish**: The fish brings love and blessing to one's home. Goldfish would attract money and wealth. A fish in a newlywed couple's house would ensure fertility. It also offsets negative energy, thereby helping to strengthen the relationship.

- **Frog**: If you like company, keep a frog in the garden if you cannot bear it inside the house.

*Man's best friend is easily spooked by ghosts and spirits, or so the Chinese believe, the next time ol'Spot starts howling, place your shoe rightside down.*

This slimy amphibian is said to attract new friends and acquaintances to a home. A frog hopping into one's home is a good omen. Each hop means one dose of good luck. If you kill a frog, other than for food, bad luck will dog you.

- **Lizard**: Lizards are believed to ward off diseases.

- **Monkey**: Keep an agile monkey as a pet and you will be rewarded with health, success and good fortune.

- **Owl**: Famed for its wisdom, this bird is feared by man as an omen of death. However, the Chinese also believe that the owl imparts intelligence and watchfulness to a household.

- **Parrot**: Besides providing entertainment to the owner, the parrot also imparts wit. Whenever the parrot whistles, close your windows because it means that it will rain soon.

- **Spider**: To have a spider is to have a web of protection around the house. The dexterity of the spider in spinning and weaving leads the Chinese to belicve that it also bestows intelligence to the owner.

*To have a spider is to have a web of protection around the house. The dexterity of the spider leads the Chinese to believe that it also bestows intelligence to the owner.*

# 58. Signs from Above

The sky is not mere empty space to geomancers who in the course of their work sometimes look to the sky for signs. Men may differ but universal is the belief that birds' patterns of flight can be a good or bad omen. Let us examine the roots of some of these superstitions.

- **Albatross:** Encountering the albatross brings good fortune.
- **Bat:** A flying bat foretells bad luck and disease. However, if a bat flies into your house, you can expect lots of gossip about you.

- **Black bird:** A black bird means having two love relationships.
- **Cock**: A cock gives warning of upcoming treachery.
- **Cuckoo**: A cuckoo's call warns husbands of their wives' infidelity. This tale has its roots in the cuckoo's habit to leave its eggs in the nest of other birds. But the Welsh believe that hearing the bird's call brings good luck if you are standing on grass, bad luck if you are on stone.
- **Dove**: A dove in the sky heralds the coming of peace.
- **Eagle:** The eagle symbolises strength, intelligence and the spirit to triumph. Seeing one soaring in the sky means your status will improve. But seeing a rapacious and ferocious eagle means you may contract a disease. Worse, if you see a dead eagle, it means all hope is lost.
- **Goose:** A goose crossing your path denotes success and riches in life.
- **Gull:** To sailors and fishermen, gulls that perch on their vessels are the souls of dead seamen.

- **Magpie:** Sighting a magpie is to expect sorrow. Sighting two means happiness is on the way. If you are pregnant, seeing three means your baby will be a girl, while four means it is a boy. If you happen to see five magpies, you can hope to find silver. Six means you will strike gold.
- **Nightingale:** Good news is expected.
- **Owl:** The owl is a bird of the night. Seeing one is bad omen, as it foretells sickness, poverty and imprisonment.
- **Peacock:** If you are a businessman, sighting a peacock brings success to your trade. If you are male and single, it means your future wife will be a beauty. Single women can expect to marry a rich and good man. But widows and widowers beware, it means you will be courted by an insincere one whose tongue drips with honey.
- **Pigeon:** The sight of flying pigeons means success in your undertakings.
- **Raven:** A raven circling in the sky, pecking the window, or perched on the roof is a sign of the coming death of a loved one. Ravens in the Tower of London are protected by law because of an old belief that England will be invaded if these birds leave.
- **Robin:** At the turn of the century, robins were sighted on three occasions in the coal mines of South Wales. The sightings preceded mining disasters in which many lives were lost. Since then, the presence of robins in the mines is perceived as a sign of impending doom for the miners.
- **Swallow:** A swallow flying over you means that everything will run smoothly, and even bitter quarrels can be solved. On the other hand, seeing one migrate means you will be receiving bad news.
- **Warbler:** To hear a warbler sing means good health.

So the next time you see a bird dart across the blue sky spare a moment to observe the bird, and perhaps you may grasp the message of the signature in the sky. Lastly, there is a common belief that having bird dropping land on you, although unpleasant, means good luck!

# 59. Broom Power

**D**uring the Middle Ages in Europe, the broom was thought to be the flying vehicle of witches. Sweeping and kicking up dirt and dust, it is not difficult to see how the lowly domestic tool gained its sinister reputation.

In China, the peasantry used to pray to *Sao Ching Niang* or the Lady of the Broom. This deity is believed to reside on the Broom Star or *Sao Chou* which

presides over the weather. When the rain continues for too long and threatens the destruction of crops, farmers would cut out paper images of the broom and paste them on doors and fences. This is thought to invoke the Lady of the Broom who would sweep away the storm and bring back clear skies.

The majority of Chinese today still believe that it is bad luck to sweep the house on the first day of the Lunar New Year.

They also believe that:

- Bringing an old broom into a new house would chase away the potential wealth of the location;
- Making a wish while using a new broom would make the wish come true;
- Jumping over a broom nine times within a year would enable a person to get a life partner;
- Swinging a broom over your head in the outdoors would bring the rain;
- Lightning is attracted by brooms, so putting a broom on the porch during a lightning storm would ensure that you have a lightning rod to protect the house;
- Hitting someone with a broom is to inflict bad luck on him;
- Reversing a broom and standing it against the door will prevent burglars from breaking in;
- Placing a miniature broom beneath the pillow of babies and children will block psychic attacks and nightmares;
- Stepping over a broomstick will stop the hauntings of an unfriendly ghost; and
- Sweeping the floor at night would affect your good fortune and disturb the spirits of the deceased who walk about during those hours.

When one sweeps the floor, it should never be outwards because good luck would be swept out of the house.

# 60. Choosing a House

There was a man who started his business in a humble way. Over the years he worked his way up to become a millionaire. In keeping with his status, he bought a bungalow which had been auctioned off because its owner had fallen into bad times.

The new owner proceeded to redecorate the bungalow to his liking. Not long after moving in with his family, the man's business suffered. He was plagued by one problem after another.

In another case related to feng shui, there was this very wealthy man who lived in a small double-storey terrace house. The many luxury cars parked in the compound gave away the owner's financial standing. When the man was asked why he stayed in such a modest-looking house, he answered that he had yet to find a place with a better feng shui than his present residence.

So it goes to show that if a particular house enjoys good feng shui, regardless of its size, and if its surroundings remain untouched by any new development, then chances are the house will continue to enjoy good feng shui.

This is why some people would never leave or sell their house unless they are sure that their new residence will have a better feng shui.

If you intend to buy a house, you should check up on the history of its owner. If the owner has been successful in his business endeavours, the house probably has good vibes running in harmony with feng shui. On the other hand, if the present tenants are not doing well or if the occupants quarrel a lot, then the feng shui of the house is questionable.

Good or bad fortune will always be trapped in the house and is unlikely to follow its occupants.

So if you choose a house with good feng shui, good luck and fortune are likely to surround you and your family, while bad tidings may befall you if you choose one with bad feng shui.

# 61. When to move house

In our life time, we move from one place to another. Sometimes it is because we have received a promotion or a raise. We buy a bigger house in tandem with our higher quality of life. We want to entertain in a more prestigious and acceptable setting. For others, it could be unfortunate circumstances which cause them to move house – the landlord gives notice to quit or the rent goes too high.

I once had a friend who shifted because he wanted to live near his workplace. The hassle of traffic jams was too much for him to bear.

Ironically, his company shifted premises shortly after he moved into the neighbour-hood. So, he packed up and moved again. And again, the company relocated. After the third such "coincidence", my friend realised he was like the dog who chased after its own tail in many circles. He decided to stay put and has faithfully joined the morning crawl to work ever since.

Moving into a new house is not a simple matter. Feng shui dictates that this be done only on a "good day" so that good luck follows the one who moves.

Monday is the day when one's sixth sense is at its peak. Moving house on Monday would bring you less headaches. If you shift on Tuesday, your perception and intellectual power are likely to improve. A Wednesday move results in passions of all kinds while moving on Thursday brings in a flow of wealth. Love and money would be the result of shifting on Friday. If you move on Saturday, make sure it is an old house, building or mansion. The person who moves on Sunday will find that good luck follows him in whatever he does.

# 62. Taboos on Moving House

We look into some taboos to observe when moving into a new house. Before saying goodbye to your old house, leave behind some money – it does not matter how much – so that the next tenant will enjoy good luck.

The first thing to bring into your new house is some salt, bread and uncooked rice. This is because salt represents wealth, while bread and uncooked rice symbolise food itself, to ensure that the new household will never know hunger or fall short of cash.

Next, to maintain stability in the household, bring a solid table or chair into the house. There is an indisputable rule that an old broom should not be brought into a new house, Such a broom would have been used to sweep dust and dirt, and an old broom in a new house would bring with it all the accompanying negativeness.

Should there be a delay in your moving in, cross a new mop and broom at the doorstep to guard your new house from unknown forces in your absence, until such times as your are ready to move in.

When you finally move in, throw a packet of firecrackers into the house to dispel all negative *chi* or drive away spirits.

Once you have settled down, consider throwing a house-warming party. Gifts from guests should also be placed in their respective places in the house.

# 63. Natural and Artificial High Ground

C hi: the higher one goes above the Earth's lines of magnetic energy, the more dissipated the *chi* (or lifeforce) becomes. A mountain, however, is a natural formation of the earth, and hence the planet's energy would flow through it as well.

There is a saying that if you seek spiritual enlightenment, you must leave all material goods and thoughts behind and be prepared to walk into the wilderness. Somewhere along your journey, the secrets of the universe would unfold before you.

In order to experience this kind of inspirational experience, hermits and ascetics would cast aside their materialistic lifestyles and head for a secluded place somewhere in the forest or mountains.

Perhaps up there among the clouds and lofty peaks, they will find what they have come to seek. Each person's experience of coming into contact with the infinite is a unique thing and cannot be adequately described. Today, there are still such people who embark on such private, lonely quests.

There are many more who scale the heights, not out of any desire to achieve enlightenment, but out of necessity — in places where there is over-crowding or insufficient land, they take to high rise buildings to work or stay in.

Structural engineering is so advanced nowadays that these skyscrapers can be built to incredible heights.

One factor that must be seriously considered is the wind. It is a fact that a building of 110 storeys in height, such as the World Trade Centre in New York, can sway up to 91 cm (36 inches) off the vertical during a strong wind.

Experiments in the United States have also shown that occupants of the higher floors of apartments tend to become edgy and irritable. It is theorised that the higher one goes above the Earth's lines of magnetic energy, the more dissipated the *chi* (or lifeforce) becomes.

The Earth's energy and its magnetic forces play an important role in all living things. Practitioners of taichi co-ordinate their breathing and body movements while tapping the Earth's magnetic energy. A recent experiment conducted by two physicists at Harvard University proves an interesting point with regard to the magnetic forces of the planet.

Two atomic clocks of the same sensitivity were placed at two different locations in a high rise building. One was fixed on the highest point while the other was left in the basement. After a few days, the scientists discovered that the clock on the roof was running faster than the one in the basement. The rea-

son they gave for this phe-nomenon was that the effect of the gravitational field is more intensely felt in the basement. On the roof, where the force was weaker, the clock simply worked faster.

Chinese fortune tellers would tell you a similar story — someone walking without placing this feet firmly on the ground would have a short lifespan. So if Man were to be allotted a certain lifespan, he could simply change it by going to live high up in a skyscraper. By doing so, he triggers his biological clock to move forward faster.

But what about those who go up to the mountains and live to be a ripe old age?

Don't forget that a mountain is a natural formation of the Earth, and hence the planet's energy would flow through them as well.

But those who are living in high rise buildings should bear in mind that these are artificial things which have less link with the Earth's power.

# 64. Swimming Pool and High rise

**N**ormally swimming pools are found in condominiums and apartments as part of the facilities. Generally speaking, to have one's apartment facing a swimming pool would seem good feng shui as it means facing lots of *shui* (money). On the contrary, it may not be so.

Here we take a good look at some of the illustrations of apartments and the swimming pools, whether they would bring us negative or positive results.

## 1. On the Top

Literally speaking, having water above oneself would mean to be drowning oneself. In this respect, apartments with a swimming pool above it simply means bad feng shui for the owners.

## 2. Fortune Flowing Away I

How does one know which part of the swimming pool is of the deeper end without have to jump into the pool. The best key sign is to look out for the diving spring board which obviously tells you where the deeper end is. If your apartment happens to face a swimming pool with the deeper end at the far side, expect your money to flow away from you.

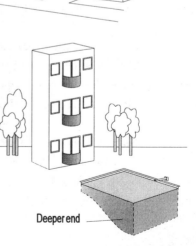

Deeper end

### 3. Fortune Flowing Away II

Another tell-tale sign that your wealth is flowing away from you is to have your apartment immediately fronting a baby's pool which obviously tells you that the pool's deeper end is at the other far side. It has the same effect.

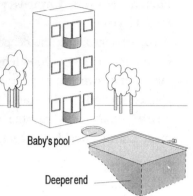

Baby's pool

Deeper end

### 4. Fortune Flowing Away III

The worst kind would be having an apartment facing a swimming pool with the deeper end at the far end linked up to a pathway. As the pathway also helps to drain one's wealth away, the intensity of one's fortune being drained away is greater.

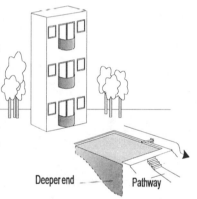

Deeper end          Pathway

### 5. Fortune Flowing Inward

If you have an apartment or condominium facing the deeper end of a swimming pool, expect lots of *shui* to flow your way.

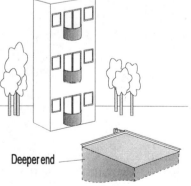

Deeper end

195

## 6. Fortune Flowing Inwards with a Secret Arrow

An apartment facing the deeper end of a pool generally is good feng shui but if the swimming pool is not aligned properly and create a secret arrow pointing towards the apartment, one's wealth is being destroyed.

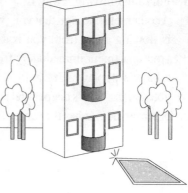

# 65. Apartment

**I**f your apartment is on the first or second floor, trees planted on the ground below your home may end up blocking your balcony. The balcony of an apartment is the outlet that provides the main view. If the view is pleasant, the residents of the apartment may prosper. But a view that is unpleasant or blocked may bring bad feng shui to the residents.

Here are several examples of blocked views and their effects:

### Fire shape
Facing the tip of pine trees — of which the shape belongs to the Fire element — will bring lots of domestic problems.

### Valley
When two trees that are close together form a valley-like view, it is bad feng shui. A valley is where strong winds blow, so to face such a view would mean having an unstable life.

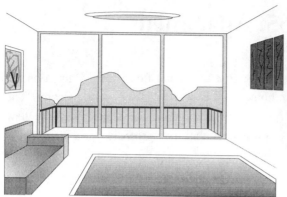

### Tree Top

If your apartment gives you a view beyond the tree top, it is good feng shui, as it symbolises your having overcome obstacles in life and ending up at the top.

### Big Tree Trunk

An apartment that faces a big tree trunk means have a big problem in one's life.

### Small Tree Trunks

An apartment that faces several small tree trunks will bring various problems to the residents.

# 66. The Balcony

The balcony of a condominium or apartment is likely to be a place where the occupants go to catch a whiff of fresh air or even to relax their tired minds. The balcony can be likened to the eye of fortune. If it faces a burial ground, hospital, police station, T-junction, temple or other places with negative vibes, then that particular apartment or condominium has bad feng shui. However, if the balcony faces a bank or financial institution, natural lake, river or even a swimming pool, then it can be said to enjoy good feng shui.

To attract good feng shui, the shape of one's balcony has to be right too. Otherwise it may repel the positive elements that come its way. Let us take a look at the various balcony shapes and see where they stand in the study of feng shui.

### Triangular Shape

As a triangle represents the fire element, a balcony shaped like a triangle will destroy whatever goodness that lies ahead.

### Arrow Shape

The arrow-shaped balcony has the same negative connotation as the triangular one, except that it is more destructive because of its sharp point facing outwards.

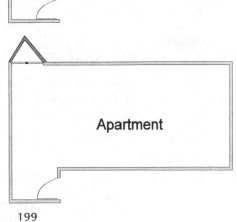

## Elegant Shape

The elegantly shaped balcony has a curve at one end. It denotes a positive nature and attracts good feng shui.

## Gold Shape

The balcony with a slanted edge on both sides is reminiscent of the ancient Chinese gold ingot. As gold symbolises wealth, a balcony shaped after a gold ingot has very positive implications.

## Long Shape

A balcony that is too long is not a well-balanced balcony as one has to walk to the far end to get a good view. Thus good fortune is elusive.

## Cup Shape

This is a good shape to have for a balcony. The empty cup can capture and retain all the good incoming vibes. If the cup-shaped balcony is located in the centre, then all the better as the whole family can benefit from it.

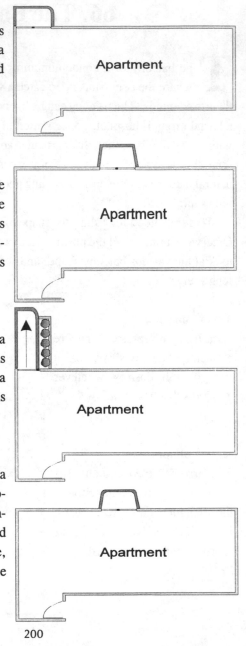

## Square Shape

Such a balcony reflects a stiff nature. Just like calling someone a square is uncomplimentary, so is having a square balcony undesirable.

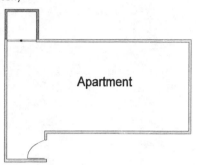

## Hidden Balcony

As this balcony is often confined within a recess, it has an introvert nature which is bad feng shui as it spells no advancement for the occupants.

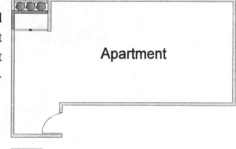

## Slanted balcony

The slant of the balcony will throw off any wealth or fortune that comes along.

## Quarter Shape

This small balcony will accommodate a single person nicely. Two would be a crowd. As the *yin* and *yang* elements cannot be balanced properly here, this is not a good balcony to have unless you are single and wish to remain so.

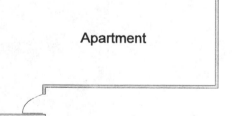

# Index

203